Bridging the Gap: Leadership Lessons for the Public Safety Leader

Anthony C. Wilson, Ph.D.

Copyright © 2015 by Anthony C. Wilson
All rights reserved. This book or any portion thereof
may not be reproduced or used in any manner whatsoever
without the express written permission of the publisher except
for the use of brief quotations in a book review.
Printed in the United States of America
First Printing, 2015
ISBN 978-1508968948
Public Safety Diversity Consultants a subsidiary of the
Hawthorne-Freeman Group
6956 E. Broad Street, Columbus, Ohio 43213
www.Publicsafetydiversity.com

Preface

Public safety organizations are hierarchical, bureaucratic organizations. As such, leaders in public safety organizations may view their organization's structure as a hindrance to their ability to lead effectively. In addition, leaders in public safety have allowed red tape to discourage them from creating a dynamic and innovative organization.

Every leader in public safety should have some knowledge of the history of those that are responsible for the manner in which public safety operates. Ben Franklin was so concerned about the devastating effects of fires on members of his community that he sought to raise public awareness about his city's need to improve firefighting techniques. Because of his leadership, the Union Fire Company was started in Philadelphia, Pennsylvania. Sir Robert Peel introduced far-ranging criminal law and prison reform in England, and is known as the father of policing after creating the first metropolitan police department. Ben Franklin and Sir Robert Peel are leaders that identified needs and sought ways to address those needs. There are great leaders that people can emulate, but today's leaders must have the ability to adapt their leadership abilities to current and future situations. There are many great leadership books and programs available for people to read, but few incorporate the dynamics of public safety organizations.

As a police sergeant with over twenty years of experience and four years as a security specialist in the United States Air Force, I have had the opportunity to interact with various leaders in different contexts. The idea of bridging the gap was birthed after witnessing first-hand the leadership divide between entry-level personnel, middle management, and executive staffs in public safety organizations. The leadership divide is what contributes to an agency's disconnect with different segments of the communities they serve. In essence, if members in the highest levels of an organization are unwilling to consider the ideas and philosophies of members from the lowest levels of an organization, then how will they effectively interact with the community?

The purpose of *Bridging the Gap* is to close the many divides that exist in public safety organizations. Bridging the gap closes the divide between executive levels of public safety organizations and members operating in the lower levels of those organizations. *Bridging the Gap* dismantles the wall that separates public safety organizations and the communities they serve. *Bridging the Gap* assists current leaders of public safety agencies by increasing their leadership capabilities. Finally, *Bridging the Gap* helps develop the leadership skills of men and women that aspire to ascend the ranks of public safety organizations.

In the mid-1990s, I conducted a leadership presentation in front of a group of MBA students that were enrolled in a leadership course. One of the questions, the students asked was whether leaders are born or made. In addition, they asked, what attributes make someone a great leader. I used to reflect back and wonder why the professor selected me to present to his class. I later realized that as an entry-level police officer, many people in the community considered those in uniform as leaders. It did not matter what rank the person was, people looked to the public safety official for guidance and direction. Many issues we see in public safety today are attributed to a lack of diversity. Diversity awareness is essential, but many issues in public safety can be attributed to a lack of leadership development throughout all levels of the organization.

The leadership presentations increased my interest in the complexities and challenges of leadership development. So much so, that I set out to pursue a doctorate with a focus on organizational leadership. During my presentations at that university, there were members of my organization who attended that were of a higher rank than I was. What separated me from them was the fact that I was very active in the community. After those leadership presentations, I soon realized that titles, educational achievements, and salary do not make an individual a good leader. I recognized that the concept of leadership is very involved and is not a one-size-fits-all approach.

Attempting to answer the question of whether leaders are made or born is tantamount to trying to determine which came first, the chicken, or the egg. Many professional leadership theorists have debated this question since the inception of the Ohio State University and University of Michigan studies on leadership behaviors and attitudes in the 1940s. Here is the simple answer to the question of whether leaders are born or made: it is obvious that all leaders are born, but good and great leaders are made. Great leadership is a result of an individual's self-motivation, aspiration, intuition, experience, and desire to be the best leader they can be.

The opportunity to contemplate various leadership trends, styles, behaviors, and theories has always intrigued me. Often highly publicized critical incidents propel an individual to the leadership apex. It is during those times that leaders are thrust into the public spotlight. Many times, the failure or success of a leader is often not realized until after he or she has left their organization or area of responsibility. Whether leading a small group or a large organization, the failure or success of a leader is often not realized until after he or she departs. That is why it is important for all leaders of an organization to spend time developing their employees and frontline supervisors. The development of those individuals will enable a great leader to live and leave a great legacy, and to achieve endless greatness.

There are those who will look at the rank of this author and immediately discard the contents of this book, which is unfortunate because one of the most important characteristics of a leader is to be teachable. *Bridging the Gap* will create a bridge that connects an organization's executive staff and middle management with their frontline supervisors and entry-level employees. Every organization has a different structure, with various formal and informal values, and a culture that espouses those values. Therefore, *Bridging the Gap* assists the leader in identifying the values that are suitable for their organization, as well the values that may hinder the organization's progress and ability to change.

Bridging the Gap will enable the current and aspiring leader to assess their ability to navigate through the various situations that a 21st-century leader will encounter. You will read some of my experiences with public safety leaders and private industry leaders, and you will learn about other people's experience with leaders in various frameworks. The last section will assist you in constructing a self-development plan as well as establishing or enhancing your personal core values. I hope you consider this book as a tool that you can place in your leadership toolbox.

Table of Contents

PREFACE 3
TABLE OF CONTENTS 7
FOREWORD 8
INTRODUCTION 10
CONNECTING LEADERSHIP 12
TRANSFORMING LEADERSHIP 19
CRISIS LEADERSHIP 34
THE L.E.A.D.E.R. PRINCIPLES 38
THE FUNDAMENTALS OF BEING A C.O.A.C.H 47
DIVERSITY: BUILDING BETTER RELATIONSHIPS 55
DISMANTLING THE WALL OF SILENCE 67
LEADER SELF-DEVELOPMENT 76
CONCLUSION 83
ABOUT THE AUTHOR 84
ADDENDUM A: LEADERSHIP 85
ADDENDUM B: PERSONAL CORE VALUES LIST 87
ADDENDUM C: LEADERSHIP VACUUM SIGNS 88
REFERENCES 90

Foreword

When Anthony C. Wilson asked me to write this foreword for his new book, *Bridging the Gap: Leadership Lessons for the Public Safety Leader*, he knew that I could evenly dissect, read, and diagnose his words NOT only as his best friend of 39 years or because we served in the military at the same time, but also because I could do so through my lens of 20 years of international disaster and local Emergency Management leadership experience. I've observed the eight-year-old kid see his dream, the teenager develop his value system over time, the young adult become a leader and maintain those values through tough personal times, and the adult excel professionally in public safety. This book is outstanding! Once you start it, you will not put it down until your public safety organization has implemented his recommendations. Some may find this book controversial; it is only controversial if you judge the contents without reading it.

Anthony or "Antman" as I affectionately call him, brilliantly maneuvers and "bridges the gap" between senior leadership, mid-level management, and staff on the ground. He explains the reality of good/poor decision-making and the consequences of not getting "buy-in" from ground-level personnel in a language that is easy for all levels of staff to follow. He connects the experiences you have had within your organization to solutions that are easily initiated through leadership. His use of real techniques, such as "the Cheeseburger approach" is stunning in its simplicity and effectiveness. This book hits hard at the common myths of public safety personnel "group think," but unlike other books similar in nature, he explains the why, what, where, and when it started; then logically walks, and in some cases, pushes the reader step-by-step up the ladder to success.

Each chapter describes an experience, its effect on internal staff, and how that affects their thinking and how it correlates to consequences in dealing with the community. Chapter 6 delves deep in discussion about the sometime "taboo" subject of diversity; how to incorporate it into your organization with the <u>TRUE</u> goal in mind of actually working toward better relationships with the community and within your organization. Anthony seamlessly continues into Chapter 7 and explores the "Blue wall of silence" and its extremely damaging consequences of losing community trust and increasing the resentfulness of your own staff. Intertwined in that powerful discussion, however, are ideas not totally new to public safety, but rather "upgraded" in terms of how public safety management has and can be changed in the future.

I believe that the principles in *Bridging the Gap* will assist any leader in public safety in recognizing potential pitfalls, as well as reengaging their staff with the community. After all, that is what public safety is here to do. In addition, those leaders who are willing to look at themselves and hear critiques of their organizations, with the added bonus of actually receiving researched and proven solutions, should read this book!

As a manager/leader, I have already begun to look at my leadership style and our organization to see how Anthony's recommendations can improve communication both internally and externally within our community.

Sulayman Brown
Assistant Coordinator, Office of Emergency Management
Fairfax County, VA

Introduction

Over the course of my studies, I have had the privilege of analyzing and examining the characteristics and behaviors of past and present leaders. Leaders such as Colin Powell, Margaret Thatcher, Alan Mulally, Angela Merkel, Bill Gates, Hilary Clinton, George W. Bush, and Rudy Giuliani have always peaked my interest. These leaders were probably inundated with questions, such as: What qualities best describe your leadership capability? What are the traits that separate you from the other managers and executives in your field? What separates you from every other leader in the world? What makes you stand out from the crowd as a leader? These are the questions every leader should be salivating to answer. Leadership is fluid; therefore, identifying a single definition, trait, or quality of a leader is nearly impossible. Various leadership styles and traits work together and complement one another, which enables the individual to become a great leader.

I have read hundreds of books on leadership and management. I have used many of the suggested leadership development techniques to become a better leader and manager. The main problem that I encountered when reading books on leadership was that very few applied to public safety. Because public safety is a hierarchical, bureaucratic entity, many leadership concepts, and theories are difficult to embrace. As a sergeant in a large law enforcement organization, many of the higher-ranking staff would not take the time to listen to my ideas because of my rank. The ball is often dropped in the public safety arena because ideas and viewpoints from the lower-ranking members of the organization are discarded.

Part of the problem in public safety is that leadership is most often identified with those in higher-ranking positions. The Federal Bureau of Investigations (FBI) or other high profile entities afford those personnel the opportunities to attend high-profile leadership academies. The problem with sending higher-ranking members to these academies is that the organization culture is already ingrained in their thinking.

If we consider that, it takes anywhere from seven to ten years or longer to attain a high-ranking position in a public safety organization. By then, the person has been through the organization socialization process multiple times and has taken on the formal and informal values of the organization. Some of those values may be contrary to the mission of public safety organizations and geared toward protecting the people within the organization as opposed to protecting members of the public. That does not mean that the leader is tainted, but it does mean that their leadership styles may be guided by the informal values of the organization, which could affect their judgment and decision-making capabilities.

The developing leader is a learner that is willing to receive fundamental instruction from anyone at any time. Many of my associates have heard me comment that the moment I stop learning is the moment I take my final breath on this earth, and even then, there will be a lesson to be learned. This book is filled with tools to assist open-minded public safety personnel in experiencing leadership in a dynamic way. *Bridging the Gap* is organized to help you choose a path of continued self and organizational development, in order to become the most well-rounded leader you can be. Yes, you can be a transformational leader in a hierarchical, bureaucratic organization. Yes, even the lowest-ranking members of public safety organizations can and should be considered leaders. Because of this, time, effort, and funding should be dedicated to the continuous development of all members of an organization, regardless of their position.

The book outlines the skills needed to transform the individual and the organization into a model of what every public safety leader and organization aspire to be. More than anything, this book will prepare the aspiring leader for all promotional interviews. Secondly, the book will assist the current leader in self-development and the development of their personnel.

Connecting Leadership

"To handle yourself, use your head; to handle others, use your heart." Eleanor Roosevelt

Connecting leadership, involves uniting team members, organizational members, and other stakeholders to achieve a shared vision. Connecting leadership has the ability to motivate members of various backgrounds to work together enthusiastically for the betterment of the organization.

Many people may disagree with the following statement: "Anyone can attempt to be a leader, but not everyone can be a good leader, and even fewer become great leaders." Many people have experienced the effects of weak leadership, including those who perceived themselves to be good leaders. The bottom line is the attitude of the leader's followers combined with the condition in which they left their area of responsibility will determine whether they were excellent, mediocre, or poor leaders. What will be your legacy when you leave your assignment or when you retire? What will the people that followed you say about your leadership effectiveness? What were the qualities that made you a good leader?

For some leaders, it is their quest for knowledge that distinguishes them as leaders, for some it is their charisma, for others it is their servant-leadership qualities. No matter what traits or qualities best describes someone as a leader, what is important is that people opted to follow them. Yes, people, peers, and subordinates choose to follow you as a leader. Despite your title, pay grade, rank, and salary; people have a choice as to whether they will allow you to lead them. The executive of a business may be in a leadership position but may not be an effective leader. If the majority of members in an organization have low morale, then whose responsibility is it to boost morale?

Low morale impacts job satisfaction, absenteeism, employee turnover, organizational commitment, trust, and leadership decisions. The efficiency and performance of an organization depend on the organizational commitment of its employees. Since leadership is one of the most decisive factors contributing to the attitudes employees have toward their organization, it is potentially one of the most obvious predictors of organizational commitment. Leadership has a substantial effect on organizational commitment (Ibrahim et al., 2010). Therefore, the role of public safety leaders is critical to the efficient operation of the organization and the performance of their personnel.

Public safety, much like the military, is a place where leaders are groomed. It is assumed that if one is working in the field of public safety then they meet the highest ethical standards, are above reproach, and are the model for leadership. Over the years, society has changed, technology has changed, new generations have entered the workforce, but the culture of public safety has been slow to keep up with many of those changes. In addition, the leadership styles of public safety managers have been slow to transform. In corporate America, the transformational leader has replaced the autocratic leader. The relations-based leader has replaced the dictator, and the situational leader has replaced the laissez-faire leader. However, in public safety, the autocrats and authoritarians are still trying to rally the troops with disconnected and over-zealously antiquated management tactics, disguised as leadership.

Titles and rank are important, but many times leaders forget about the frontline supervisors and employees until a crisis or critical incident occurs. Many leadership development, coaching, and mentoring programs in public safety are designed for those in the upper ranks, but what about those who do not aspire to rise through the ranks? Is any consideration given to frontline supervisors who aspire to lead where they are, those leaders that want to remain engaged with personnel on the ground? There are those who prefer to lead on the front line because they still feel a direct connection to the principles upon which their chosen field was established. In addition, they feel a deep connection to the entry-level employees, the civilian personnel, and the community.

Organizations should never limit leadership development and mentoring opportunities to upper-level management. By then, the organizational culture has been embedded consciously or subconsciously into the person, and if the culture is divisive, exclusive, sexist, or discriminatory, then the opportunity to change the culture is lost. Public safety organizations should start early with leadership development. Pre-promotional developmental programs, mentoring programs, and in-service training programs all provide opportunities for public safety organizations to employ leadership development training.

Recently, I learned of an encounter a supervisor had with a public safety executive. The executive was attempting to inspire the frontline supervisor to take a promotional exam. In response, the lower-ranking supervisor implied that he desired to lead from the position he was currently assigned. The executive told the supervisor that at his current rank he would not be considered a leader. Instead of accepting the supervisor's rationale for not pursuing promotional opportunities, the executive nearly destroyed the supervisor's morale. This particular supervisor took a hit in the optimism department because his perception of the conversation was that those in higher-ranking positions did not view those in the lower levels of the organization as leaders.

The problem that continues to permeate throughout public safety agencies is the notion that staff members operating in lower-level positions are incapable of leading. This perception has created a schism in the public safety culture that screams rank has its privileges. Rank does indeed have its privileges, but that does not mean it has to be at the expense of neglecting the intellect and passion of personnel in the lower levels!

When an organization does not take the time to develop its frontline supervisors, it contributes to its ineffectiveness and lack of progress. When an organization intentionally places developmental limitations on lower-ranking personnel, it creates subcultures based on rank. These subcultures may develop their own ideologies about the purpose, vision, and mission of the organization. When an organization minimizes the role of its entry-level personnel and frontline supervisors, it misses out on an opportunity to develop one of its most vital and diverse components. A title or a rank does not make you a good leader; it is how you perform with that title and rank. How a leader influences and develops their subordinates is a determination of their leadership success. How the leader acts under the authority of their rank determines their real leadership capabilities. How a leader arrives at making decisions that affect the entire organization determines the depths of their leadership skills.

I will reference the biblical story of Balaam and his donkey to make a brief point. The story of Balaam is a lesson in humility. Balaam's donkey was trying to save his life, but Balaam would not listen because he perceived that the donkey was not on his level of intelligence. Why should he (Balaam) have paid attention to the perspective of a subhuman creature (Donkey) that was incapable of giving him a good reason for what he was doing? Higher-ranking personnel must take the time to listen to lower-ranking members of the organization. In the end, the donkey ended up saving Balaam's life! In the same manner, frontline supervisors or entry-level employees can help the organization if they are given an opportunity to excel. There is a wise saying, "Everyone should be quick to listen, slow to speak, and slow to become angry." Good leaders, above all, should model these words of wisdom and not be afraid to exhibit a spirit of humility.

Everyone has weaknesses; therefore, if a subordinate or junior-ranking individual (even one below your status, your education level, or your age) ends up between you and what you perceive to be crucial, try following these three suggestions: Reverence their motivations even if you do not understand or you disagree. Listen to their perspective and try to consider their viewpoint on what the risk might be. Whatever you do, do not hit (verbally assault) them in anger just because they stand between you and what you perceive as important. If anything, it is better to be too diplomatic than too disparaging.

The public safety manager should recognize that frontline supervisors and members at the entry-level ranks are just as vital to the organization as personnel in the upper levels. Public safety executives must continually iterate the importance of the entry-level employees and frontline supervisors to the rest of the group. This should not occur immediately following a critical incident, or at some special awards or recognition program, but should happen on a continual basis. This will be illustrated in one of the later sections of the book, titled "Becoming a C.O.A.C.H."

Many years ago, I read a quote that said, "If you want to know what type of a leader someone is, just pay attention to how their personnel react when he or she enters a room." If you were to walk into a room filled with your subordinates and peers what would they say about you? Would they make eye contact with you or would they intentionally look in a different direction? Would they happily greet you or would they go out of their way to avoid you? I am not referring to your inner circle, but members at various levels of your organization. Mike Myatt said, the best leaders are effortless and adaptable in their approach. They understand the power of, and the necessity for relative leadership. Contextual leadership is being able to adapt to your environment by having the ability to communicate well with varying personalities inside and outside of the organization. Good leadership programs and training will enable your organization to continue developing quality leaders well into the future.

Vision, not Visibility

Leaders must pursue the organization's mission and not their personal agenda. Leadership does not feed egos; it keeps egos in check. Good leadership skills keep you grounded, focused, and prepared. Great leaders are passionate about what they do and convey that passion and enjoyment to the rest of their team. Without passion, leaders will find it difficult to motivate their personnel. The passion of leaders is evident by the way they approach their work. In particular, a passionate leader has positive body language, upbeat communication, and timely use of optimistic verbal skills.

Leaders that are constantly in the lens of the media cameras are visibility seekers. The role of public information and public affairs personnel is to interact with the media. The regular members appreciate your presence at critical incidents, but the key is to allow everyone to perform their role without interference or interruption. This allows for a smooth flow of communication up and down the levels of the organization. Many public safety websites display photos and bios of the chief and executive staff on their home page. This is great, but a biography is not the first thing a person should see when they visit a public safety website. Judge and Robbins (2010) state those with a high achievement need are interested in how well they do personally and not in influencing others to do well. If someone is visiting your organization's website, he or she is not looking for bios and career achievements; they are most likely searching for other pertinent information.

Several years ago, fear gripped the citizens of Southern Franklin County, Ohio, because of a highway shooter that was branded the "I-270 shooter." The county sheriff had jurisdiction over the incident, and his office conducted multiple press conferences to update the media and the community on the progress of the investigation. At every press conference, the sheriff, albeit popular, rarely spoke to the media about the investigation. The task was given to his Chief Deputy and remained with the Chief Deputy until the shooter was apprehended.

The actions of the local sheriff provide insight into how leaders might run an organized and efficient operation. The organization's mission was the priority, and personal visibility was inconsequential to the sheriff. There were no blurred lines of communication, and although the sheriff was not briefing the media, everyone knew that he was still in charge. Be aware of leaders who desire to be in front of the camera, because inevitably what they are saying is, "At this moment, it is about me." When this occurs, personal visibility has taken the place of the vision and the mission of the organization.

Transforming Leadership

"The mediocre leader tells. The good leader explains. The superior leader demonstrates. The great leader inspires." William Arthur Ward

The *Merriam-Webster* dictionary defines *transform* as follows: "To change completely, usually in a good way." If you have ever seen the 2009 movie "Transformers: Revenge of the Fallen," you will recall that famous quote made by Optimus Prime, "Fate rarely calls upon us at a moment of our choosing." This quote defines the spirit of leadership and the willingness to forge ahead when it is most difficult. Transformational leadership may not be an easy concept to implement in a government or bureaucratic setting, but it is the key to moving hierarchal organizations into the 21st century. Transformational leadership is the style that current and upcoming generations will recognize. Transformational leadership is an inclusive, innovative, and creative style that compels people to follow.

Public safety in the traditional sense is often devoid of modern types of leadership styles. Most of us have encountered leaders who demanded perfection and respect, but lacked regard for their followers. Transformational leadership is contrary to the leadership methods often found in public safety agencies. Bass and Riggio (2006) describe *transformational leadership* as, the ability to inspire followers to unite with a shared vision and goals, challenging them to be innovative problem solvers by coaching, mentoring, and providing for them.

Let us be clear that there is not one way to inspire followers, and it does take time for the leader to get to know their personnel. It may take time to understand what motivates people and compels them to exceed their own expectations. A good leader will spend quality time with their subordinates to gain more clarity on what they value the most. Quality time with subordinates is what will assist the leader in keeping their personnel motivated. What are your personnel passionate about? What are they focused on? How do you get them to perform at their maximum capacity?

It is hard to understand how a supervisor or manager can spend so much time with their personnel, but never have a desire to assist in their development as leaders. Often these managers devote more time trying to tear down people instead of building them up. Another example is the supervisor who only attempts to develop those with whom they have a "good" relationship. This is unfortunate because many leaders have failed their personnel in the area of leadership development because the leader favored certain staff members over others. This book is about implementing modern leadership styles in tradition-laden organizations. These leadership styles should not be viewed as the clashing of old styles with the new, but more of a fusion of the two.

Transformational is cutting edge as it applies to leadership in a hierarchal organization; it is stepping outside of the leadership box and creating innovative methods to enhance the effectiveness of yourself and your organization. Transformational leadership in the public safety arena stresses the importance of leading where you are. You can be an entry-level employee, patrol officer, deputy, trooper, firefighter, EMT, or a low-ranking enlisted soldier, marine, sailor, or airman, and still be a great leader. Bass and Riggio (2006) identify transformational leaders as those with the ability to motivate others to do more than they originally intended and often even more than believed possible. That explanation of transformational leaders is an excellent description of the characteristics *every* leader should possess!

There has been much debate on whether there is a difference between leadership and management. Here is an insight into what I see as the difference between leaders and managers. Do not focus on the terms *manager* and *leader*, but concentrate on the act of managing and the act of leading. A manager is one who manages or tends to the present situation. They can be decisive when they have to, they rarely take risks, and will only be all in, when there are minimal risks. A leader is one who has foresight and is not afraid to be innovative and think outside of the box. A leader sees what is ahead and prepares for it. A leader will be decisive in all matters, especially in moment decisions. It is possible for a person to possess manager and leader traits at the same time. Managing and leading at the same time is the core of situational leadership, which involves adapting leader and manager styles to the development level of the persons they are trying to lead. Not everyone is willing to follow a leader, but every situation involving followers can be successfully managed!

A leader can be described as a person who has decided to move out into the forefront. The leader will exhibit qualities that inspire people to follow them. Another great disservice that has saturated the public safety profession is the push for pseudo-leadership development programs. It is good when public safety agencies want to develop leaders, but when this training is conducted in-house, it often involves the higher-ranking officials of that organization enforcing their perception of the skills a leader must possess. In essence, you may have weak leaders attempting to inspire members of an organization to emulate their leadership characteristics. Additionally, you may have leaders who are so disconnected from the front lines that they alienate personnel because of their lack of awareness.

Leadership development and training is estimated to cost $10–50 billion a year, yet its effectiveness is unclear and transfer to the agency remains a challenge (Kerschreiter et al., 2012). There are many reasons attributed to this problem. An important issue is that traditional leadership development has often focused on the leader as a person. The aim of the traditional method is to change leaders' behavior to fit a predefined governing model of what a leader should be (Ford & Harding, 2007). However, this ignores the wider context of leadership in which leaders operate (Day, 2001), including the role of followers in the leadership development process. Leadership development programs must consider the culture of the organization, the morale of the personnel within the organization, and the overall attitude of the employees.

Many agencies will say their development process is different, but if the agency's mission, vision, purpose, core values, and goals are not a part of the development, then the training is not reflective of the organization's beliefs. According to Burnette et al. (2012), leadership success is not achieved by oneself, but often by looking to other successful individuals, and role models, for inspiration and motivation.

Leadership success is not attributed to the achievement of a high-ranking position or title. An attribute of leader success is the amount of people who enthusiastically follow the leader. The number of leaders that were developed under the leader's watch is another indicator of leadership success. When we look at those that have been tasked with teaching leadership development in the public safety arena; we have to ask the question, other than a title, what are their achievements? How do *they* interact with the community? What do the internal and the external stakeholders say about them?

Since there are multiple definitions of leadership, the public safety agency must be careful about pressuring people to read leadership books. Members of an organization must be leery of the executive that makes particular leadership books required reading. Books on leadership should be approached as a means of self-development. When an executive is shoving multiple leadership books in front of their staff, it can create mass confusion, especially if the books involve various leadership theories and principles.

Another issue that can develop when the executives force leadership manuals on their personnel is the executive may have a particular management style that they want their followers to emulate. Unfortunately, what works for one manager may not work for other managers because the behavior and attitudes of their personnel will differ. In addition, leadership approaches may differ at various levels of hierarchical organizations, which may create further problems. That is why training on leadership has to be tailored to meet the needs of particular industries.

Since there are many external and internal variables that impact the way a person manages, the good manager/leader must be able to adapt their style to the situation. Fred Fiedler developed the *contingency theory*; this theory pointed out that leadership effectiveness is the result of the interaction between the style of the leader and the characteristics of the environment in which the leader works. If an executive is shoving leadership books down the throats of their personnel, then that is a good indication that the manager themselves, may want to spend more time in leadership self-development, as opposed to having everyone conform to his or her leadership style.

In training, I like to use an illustration of the Christian Bible to make a single point. When most people read the Bible, they do not reflect, but they deflect. They do not see individual weaknesses as applying to their leadership skills, but see those weaknesses as applying to others. When leaders read articles and books on leadership and fail to take time to reflect on their leadership weaknesses, they miss the opportunity to fulfill the intent of the literature. Thus, more leaders should focus on 360-degree feedback as a way to foster self-development.

When reading a book designed for self-development, the reader should see their image reflected in the book, if they do not see their image, then the book is telling them that they need to change or update their leadership methods. If the book suggests a certain way to engage your personnel and that approach appears foreign to you, then it is an opportunity to try it out, even if you have to tailor the method to fit your organization's structure.

Another mistake that is often made by public safety agencies is that their leadership development programs are members-only events. Leader development should not be limited to those in the upper echelon. Leader development should occur at all levels of the organization. In public safety, the military, and many other organizations, the entry-level ranks should be introduced to various aspects of leadership. Members at all level of an organization should be given the opportunity to participate in various profiles, such as the DISC leadership profile and MBTI personality profile. These are not only beneficial for the mid-level and upper-level management, but are good for the early development of entry-level employees.

Here is another illustration of leaders and managers. Those familiar with the game of professional football, specifically American football, will grasp this concept. Let us consider the position of quarterback in this illustration. Argumentatively the quarterback position is the most vital role on the team. The quarterback touches the ball nearly every play that the offense is on the field. They have enormous responsibilities in calling plays, changing the play before the ball is put in play, and making moment decisions within the context of those plays.

In football, we often hear of quarterbacks being game managers or leaders. A game manager is the quarterback that does not try to do too much. They will not make many mistakes because they will not take any unnecessary risks. The problem with the game manager is that no one on offense ever reaches their full potential, because they are particularly meticulous in how they approach the game. The game manager will win and can be successful. Thus, the manager may improve some of the people around them, but those people may never reach their full potential. They will get the job done, but in a manner that will not separate them from the rest of the organization.

The manager will make minimal mistakes, but their team may become stagnant and predictable. In contrast, the good leaders are the Joe Montana's, Steve Young's, Tom Brady's, Drew Brees', and the Manning's of football. These quarterbacks are representative of leaders who take chances; they improvise, are innovative and creative. Good leaders will always seek to make everyone around them better. How would Jerry Rice have fared without a Joe Montana or a Steve Young? Because of their leadership abilities, many of these leaders have contributed to the induction of members of their team into the professional football hall of fame.

A final illustration is a quarterback by the name of Trent Dilfer. Trent Dilfer won a Superbowl with the Baltimore Ravens, and throughout the season, he merely managed the team all the way to the championship. In fact, the Baltimore Ravens offense was average, ranking 14 out of 31 teams that year. However, the Baltimore Ravens had the top defense in the National Football League. General Colin Powell once said, "Management is easy. Leadership is engaging and motivating people, turning people on, getting 110% out of a personal relationship." Very few people have the ability to get 110% out of their people, often maybe 10% can succeed at this, but if the other 90% can be good managers and can get 100% out of a personal relationship, then the organization as a whole becomes extremely successful. Trent Dilfer will always be a winning Superbowl quarterback because of his *management* ability to get 100%, but Ray Lewis will be in the hall of fame because of his ability to get the additional 10% out of his people.

Good leaders are remembered because they not only transform themselves, but they transform those around them to include the entire organization. The legacy the leader leaves can be bad or good, but the good manager will leave the position the way they found it, still productive, but with few lasting changes. Finally, leaders leave legacies, and managers leave jobs. In summary, leadership and management are very similar in concept. You can be a good or bad leader, just as you can be a good or bad manager. In the end, it is important that you transform yourself and your organization into a more proficient and modern institute.

If leadership development and training is estimated to cost $10–50 billion a year, yet its effectiveness is unclear, then the organization must create techniques to measure its effectiveness or develop a viable alternative method. Those adjustments will enable the organization to get the most out of developing current and future leaders of their organizations.

The Act of Leading

There are many ways to describe leadership. To narrow it down to a simple definition would do a disservice to all of the significant past, present, and future leaders in the world. Leadership is not a term or a title, but it is an act. Many will promote themselves as leaders, but few will act the part. The introduction stated that leadership is not about titles, pay grades, and positions. Bernie Madoff was the founder and CEO of his company, but that did not make him a good leader. He had the title and the pay that came with the title, but not the mindset of a leader.

Kenneth Lay the CEO and vice president of Enron had the titles, but apparently, he did not exhibit good leadership qualities. Instead of trying to describe leadership, it may be just as pertinent to focus on what leadership is not.

In some of the classes I have taught on leadership, I often ask participants to name a leader from the past or present they admire and list one quality that makes them a good leader. Once everyone has selected his or her leader and the identifying quality, we poll the entire class and narrow our leaders down to one or two that possess all of the qualities listed on the board. Then we begin the development process with those in the class by discussing in detail the experiences and concepts of that particular leader, and how those experiences and concepts molded the person into a great leader. Whether it was combat, crisis, or conflict; the individual emerged from the situation with the reputation of being an excellent leader.

Again, leadership is not a title. Just because you have a title does not make you a leader. Your title can be Officer, Firefighter, Deputy, Corporal, Sergeant, Lieutenant, Captain, Commander, Assistant Chief, Deputy Chief, and Chief! It only means you have earned a title, but what you do under the auspices of that title determines whether you are considered a good leader or not. I have seen more patrol officers, firefighters, TSA agents, and other entry-level employees exhibit more leadership attributes than many of their superiors.

How do many of the leadership experts describe the act of leading? John Maxwell says, "Leadership is a process not a position." Ken Blanchard says leadership is "the capacity to influence others by unleashing their power and potential to impact the greater good." General George C. Marshall said, "When we are tired, cold and hungry, at the end of the day, it is the leader who puts aside his personal discomfort to look to the needs of his soldiers." Colin Powell describes leadership, as "the art of routinely accomplishing more than the science of management says is possible."

In the public safety arena, leadership is much more than a title, rank, a fancy position, or an elevated position on the wage scale. Leadership is the ability to elevate everyone around you. It is moving self out of the way for the greater good of the organization. If your personal mission and desires outweigh those of the organization, then your reputation as a leader is in grave jeopardy.

Leading Where You Are

In the arena of public safety, it is difficult for many to fathom that entry-level personnel can be considered leaders. Because of that belief, the leadership abilities of many frontline supervisors can be hindered. The obstruction occurs because those in the upper ranks want to control the outcome of situations to enhance their credibility. For the good leader, it is not important to receive accolades or attain glory; ultimately, what matters most is to leave at the end of each day feeling as if you have positively impacted your subordinates, your peers, your organization, and your customers.

Public safety leaders understand that their position requires more from them because they hold a position of public trust. Leading where you are is having the ability to employ leadership skills in your current rank. For example, a police officer or firefighter can be a leader and elevate everyone around them, including their superiors.

Here are two examples of what can be accomplished if one chooses to lead from where they are. First, as a patrol supervisor it was my goal to influence people to function to the best of their ability. I implemented officer of the month programs at my expense. The officers were not competing against one another, but they were acknowledged for their outstanding contribution to the organization and the community. When you suspect that morale is low and upper management does not recognize personnel for their hard work, then it is the responsibility of middle management and the frontline supervisor to acknowledge the contributions of their staff. In this case, officers were acknowledged for taking the initiative to address problems in their areas of responsibility. They were recognized for their contribution to the community in which they served. Some would volunteer in the community on their own time to mentor youth or coach sports teams. In public safety, these leadership traits must be recognized and continuously praised.

When you consider the qualities that make people good leaders, you and your staff should have a desire to possess the attributes to serve the community in various capacities. When you lead where you are, you seek ways to develop personnel so that they will display positive leadership qualities that will benefit the organization long after you are gone.

Second, in my fifth year as a patrol supervisor, there were two precincts operating out of a small building. The city provided $1.4 million in funding so a new building could be constructed to house the two precincts. There were five other supervisors and three higher-ranking personnel operating out of that cramped building. As time went on, there seemed to be a lack of initiative on anyone's part to manage the project. After a few months, it was rumored that a high-ranking city official wanted to construct the new building in an area that was not suitable for either precinct. Once I heard this, I immediately forwarded a letter to the appropriate authority requesting permission to take charge of the project. After a series of conversations between various entities, I was allowed to proceed with the project.

As a frontline supervisor heading up a $1.4 million project, I was able to lead from where I was. In the end, I located a suitable property, and the new building was constructed with enough room to accommodate the two precincts and a community center. At the groundbreaking ceremony, it was exciting to stand in the background as city and community leaders broke ground. A few years later at the ribbon cutting ceremony, I again stood in the background as the dignitaries cut the ribbon. Here is the point; I did not want the credit or the glory, I only wished to see the project completed, because it would benefit the personnel that were tasked with serving the citizens in that particular community. It was not about me; it was about taking the initiative for the greater good of the personnel and the organization. I am very proud of that accomplishment and can leave knowing that I did not merely leave a position, but I left a legacy.

The above examples show that it does not take the most intelligent, charismatic, and highest-ranking person to lead. Leading requires desire, passion, self-confidence, and a willingness to succeed.

Leadership Training

Field training officers (FTO) and those that conduct on-the-job training for new members of an organization are leaders; however, these individuals rarely receive any leadership development training. If you poll most training officers on whether they have received any leadership training, most will respond with a resounding, No! Why? Because most are "just" patrol officers; they have no fancy titles, but they have the responsibility of training, coaching, and mentoring new officers. Do you remember the quarterback's responsibilities? They have enormous responsibilities in calling plays and making moment decisions within the context of those plays. The training officer has enormous personal and organizational responsibilities like that of the quarterback.

A training officer is tasked with moment decisions that could not only determine their fate, but the fate of their trainee. The training officer is likely to encounter many ethical dilemmas. To correctly respond to those dilemmas, the organization should assist their training officers in the development of Personal Core Values (PCV's). Personal Core Values (PCV's) are those guiding principles that assist in circumstances when the core values of the organization may not be applicable. Until the day they retire, the training officer remains a role model and a mentor to every officer they have trained. The trainee never forgets their trainer, and they always remember how they were taught, whether it was perceived as good, bad, or ugly.

Much like the Field Training Officer, entry-level public safety personnel are leaders but many have never received leadership development training. These men and women are tasked with life altering moment decisions. They are often the face of the organization; they are the customer service reps, counselors, babysitters, and unlicensed psychologists. When everyone is running away from the problem, public safety personnel are running toward it.

Most people can remember having a supervisor that could not make moment decisions. They always had to refer to the policy/procedure book that had all of the answers. The problem that befalls these types of supervisors occurs when particular problems or situations are not in the book. The dreaded gray area is where a manager may stumble, but it is where every leader thrives. How many times have you witnessed someone lose their ability to function because of a gray area? They become indecisive and often will defer to someone with a higher rank to make the decision for them. These may not be decisions that need to be made during a crisis but are instances where common sense and a little ingenuity would have saved time and effort.

Leadership involves decision-making, and when leaders fail, it is not because they made a right or wrong decision, but mainly because they failed to make any decision. There are many reasons why this happens but often it is that they are concerned about the repercussions of making a wrong decision. What would have happened if President John F. Kennedy had made no decision during the Cuban missile crisis? What if during the September 11, 2001, terrorist attacks the passengers on United Airlines Flight 93 would have made no decision? Leadership requires making a moment decision without concern for being wrong because innately the leader knows something has to be accomplished!

The Cheeseburger Approach

Organizations are much like layers in a cheeseburger. They have layers or levels that serve a purpose. You have the CEO or chief, which is the top bun. You have the executive staff, which we will call the cheese. You have middle management, which is the actual burger. Finally, you have the front-line supervisors and entry-level employees, which are the bottom bun; yes, the bottom bun!

When we look at a cheeseburger, the first thing we see is the top bun. The top bun is the attention getter. If the top bun looks good, we assume the whole burger will probably be good. There is a reason top buns are distinctively different from the bottom buns. If the top bun looks bad, one will assume the rest of the burger is tainted.

The second layer is the cheese. Simply put, the cheese is what makes it a cheeseburger, but often if the cheese on a burger is bad; we tend to scrape it off and only go with a regular hamburger. Executive staffs are very critical, but one must ask the question; would an organization survive without its executive staff? The chief or CEO may think the organization would not survive, but if we consider the matter in all sincerity; most people will agree that any organization can survive by reducing executive staffing levels. Companies survive every day by reducing the number of personnel at various levels of an organization. Clearly, the company's survival depends on the development of the staff at the lower levels that remain.

The third layer is the burger. The burger provides the flavor; it can make or break the sandwich. Middle management would be described as the burger. It plays a vital role in how the organization is perceived internally and externally. A bad burger destroys the reputation of the organization that created the burger. Middle management can be destructive if they are not in line with organizational values. If middle management fails to adhere to the mission and vision of the agency, then the organization as a whole will suffer.

The fourth layer is the forgotten level of the burger. This is the bottom bun. Most people never pay attention to the bottom bun unless something is wrong with it. The bottom bun is rarely in one's initial sight or thoughts when looking at a burger. The bottom buns are the frontline supervisors and entry-level employees. They are the entry-level civilian employees in the public safety field. They are the patrol officers, firefighters, deputies, corporals, sergeants, dispatchers, record keepers, payroll clerks, and everyone else on the front line. They are the real ambassadors of the organization because they communicate daily with the investors (citizens) and the customers (citizens).

The chief/CEO, executive staff, and middle management can go a full day or more without having any contact with the outside world, while the bottom bun is in constant communication with society. They see and understand the constant changes that occur in the communities they serve. When we pick up a cheeseburger, we do not notice anything about the bottom bun unless there is a problem with it. We pay no attention to it when it is sitting on the plate. When inspecting our cheeseburger it is the most neglected part. However, when the bottom bun is hard or mushy, it becomes an issue to us. In fact, for most people, it ruins their desire to consume the burger.

In many organizations, the frontline supervisors and entry-level employees are often neglected in the area of leadership development. There is a centralized structure where all of the decisions are made at the top; very little input is provided by middle management and frontline supervisors, even though Mintzberg (2011) suggests that middle managers are often better at leveraging the informal network of an organization that enables it to make permanent change possible. The lack of involvement by middle management and frontline supervisors creates an environment of mistrust and the perception of incompetence amongst upper-level management and personnel at the lower levels.

The top corporations in world understand the importance of the bottom bun. These organizations know that if the bottom bun is good, then more than likely the entire cheeseburger is going to be good. Visit any fortune 500 company's website, and you will see the commitment to their entry-level employees, as well as their commitment to diversity. Now randomly go to a public safety website, and you will observe a different dynamic taking place. Public safety agencies often fail in their efforts to publicly promote their commitment to the lower ranks, and in turn fail in their recruitment efforts.

More than likely if you visit a public safety agency's website you will see a photo of their top executive. Alongside the photo will be a few paragraphs on their rise through the ranks. If the organization would place entry-level employees or frontline supervisors on the website, it would create a more inclusive environment. Photos of entry-level employees along with comments on how the organization has contributed to their self-development have the potential to create a recruitment windfall.

The next time you sit down to have a cheeseburger or any other type of sandwich on a bun, turn it upside down and see if it is evenly supported. In all likelihood, it will lean in one direction and may even fall apart. When the cheeseburger is placed right side up, it supports the entire weight of the burger, the cheese, and the top bun. Thus, many organizations should be appreciative of those who are the foundation of the whole organization.

An additional point is that just because the top bun looks good does not necessarily mean the entire burger will be good. The head of an organization will most often be the face of that organization. They are believed to be the organization's ambassador to their customers and investors. They will say all of the right things and ensure they adhere to political correctness, but the real ambassadors are those who communicate with and interact with all segments of the community on a daily basis. Good leaders lead and influence people primarily based on persuasion through excellent social process skills (Burke, MacDonald, & Stewart, 2006). In essence, people are influenced by the relational skills of those charged with leading them.

What do your peers and subordinates say when you enter the room? Does the room go completely silent, or are people genuinely happy to see you and to be in your presence? People's actions and attitudes will speak volumes as to whether you are perceived as a good leader.

Crisis Leadership

"Leadership is not about titles, positions, or flow charts. It is about one life influencing another." John C. Maxwell

As a former member of my agency's crisis negotiation team, I have had the privilege of observing the actions of my team leaders during precarious times. In addition, I have been fortunate enough to interact with the leadership and members of various Special Weapons and Tactics (SWAT) teams. My interaction with these leaders has strengthened my awareness of the importance of crisis leadership.

Research on crisis leadership has primarily involved the observation of leaders during perilous events. Based on those observations, researchers identified appropriate leader behaviors during crises. A *crisis* is a high-stress situation that requires decisiveness and immediate action. *Crisis leadership* is the actions taken in response to a high-stress situation. This section will address three areas that are critical for leaders during times of crisis. These areas are self-awareness, situational awareness, and social awareness.

Leaders who find themselves in a crisis must be keenly aware of the circumstances that gave rise to the situation. In essence, the leader has to be cognizant of all elements of the situation. Although being aware of the situation is a no-brainer to most leaders, unfortunately, most of us have learned lessons of leadership through the failure and mistakes of others. Many people may not remember the great things Captain Edward J. Smith may have accomplished, but they remain aware of the fate of the Titanic. Over 100 years later, the Titanic still rests on the bottom of the ocean because of failed leadership. It took two years to build the "unsinkable" Titanic, but in a matter of hours, an iceberg managed to send it to its demise.

The captain of the Titanic failed to heed at least seven warnings from passing ships of the dangerous icebergs that were forming in the ocean. He also failed to give the order to slow the ship as they were approaching the area containing the icebergs. Finally, the captain of the Titanic canceled a lifeboat drill the day the ship hit the iceberg. The cancellation of the lifeboat drill may be directly attributed to the loss of over 1,500 lives in that unfortunate accident.

Situational Awareness

Situational awareness is the capability of the leader to recognize, process, and understand the critical elements of information concerning the situation. During a time of crisis, leaders must identify the problem and consider multiple approaches on how to address the problem. Crises often bring the leader face-to-face with a situation they have never encountered before. In the midst of these circumstances, there may be questions to which the manager does not know the answers.

An active crisis leader will most often live on the front end of reality. The leader will have the ability to identify the significance of what is taking place and not be moved by the consequences. Situational awareness is the ability to see the big picture. These leaders can see all of the moving parts of the crisis and understand what the cause and effect is.

A crisis is fluid and contains many variables. The astute leader will understand the importance of teamwork in crises. In these situations, leaders have to be willing to consider the ideas and perceptions of others. The astute leader will gather opposing viewpoints from individuals with whom they might not agree, but respect. The opposing viewpoints may lead to the creation of solutions that may not have been previously considered. If the opposing view is the best solution, the strong leader will be prepared to implement it and assume the risk.

Self-Awareness

Self-awareness is being conscious of what you do well and having the ability to acknowledge what it is you still have to learn. This involves admitting when you do not have the solution to a problem. The leader that practices self-awareness will engage others in brainstorming for potential solutions, even though they may have a desired resolution in mind.

Successful leaders are those that possess self-awareness and are confident enough to accept that their way may not be the best way. Unsuccessful leaders will only listen to those who agree with them and will often encourage simple-minded thinking. The successful crisis leader will seek out team members who have a different perspective on an issue.

In an interview with CEO Coach Eric Holtzclaw, Dave Brookmire stated, "Most leaders that fail, fail to get feedback." Strong leaders will continuously evaluate themselves and will solicit feedback from peers and subordinates as a means to improve their leadership skills. During a debriefing immediately following a crisis incident, I have seen team leaders conduct a self-analysis in front of the group.

These leaders then proceeded to ask for feedback on what they could have done better. During the course of receiving the feedback, they acknowledged certain areas that needed to be strengthened. This is an example of leader self-awareness. These leaders have a desire to do better. Because they aspire to do their best, their team will always perform at a high level.

A mistake that I have personally witnessed from people in leadership positions is their inability to control their emotions. The lack of emotional control in a crisis can destroy a team's morale and motivation. A leader that exhibits self-awareness will recognize that their emotions are trying to take over. If you feel your emotions creeping into the situation, slow down and take a deep breath. When you experience anger, frustration, or other strong emotions, slow down to examine why.

Remember, no matter how difficult the situation, you always have a choice as to how you react to it. Uncontrolled emotions have no intelligence. When emotions take over, the ability to make good decisions is affected.

One of the ways a leader can improve their self-awareness is to keep a journal. If you spend just a few minutes each day writing down your thoughts, this can move you to a higher degree of self-awareness.

Social Awareness

The supportive leader will exhibit social awareness. *Social awareness* is recognizing others' feelings, needs, and concerns. Social awareness is necessary for crisis leadership because it affects how a leader responds to people and situations. Primarily, social awareness is about carefully considering what people want and planning to communicate with them in a way that is intended to meet that need.

Crisis leadership involves getting the team to function efficiently in a moment situation. A leader that is socially aware will be sensitive to and understand the viewpoints of others. They will understand the needs and concerns of persons on each side of the situation. For example, a leader that practices social awareness will listen intently and pay attention to emotional cues. They will understand the needs of members of the community and attempt to match those needs with the appropriate services.

A leader that possesses social awareness understands the importance of empathy, organizational awareness, and service. Social awareness requires the leader to understand the politics within their organization and how those politics affect their members. Social awareness is carefully considering the needs of people and communicating with them in a manner that will help meet those needs.

The inability to effectively lead during a crisis will haunt a leader throughout their career. That is why it is vital for every member of an organization to constantly seek ways to develop their leadership skills. Remember, the Titanic remains at the bottom of the sea because a leader failed to heed warnings and to take appropriate action.

The L.E.A.D.E.R. Principles

"The greatest leader is not necessarily the one who does the greatest things. He is the one that gets the people to do the greatest things."
Ronald Reagan

The L.E.A.D.E.R. principles are designed to provide the current and aspiring leader with a set of guidelines that are easy to reference and adhere to. The principles establish a foundation upon which the manager can build upon. The L.E.A.D.E.R. principles will help any leader align themselves with the vision and mission of any organization. They are universal rules that enable the manager to maintain focus, in addition to sustaining their credibility and integrity.

Loyalty

I use former Secretary of State Hilary Clinton in this section despite the fact that many may not envision her as a leader. Let us look at Mrs. Clinton outside of her stint as the first lady and wife of a two-term U.S. President. Let us examine Hilary Clinton in the context of her 2008 run for the Democratic presidential nomination. Many popular political pundits assumed that Hilary Clinton would receive the nomination to represent the Democratic Party in the 2008 presidential election. It was shocking to many people when she lost to an upstart senator from the state of Illinois.

What separated Hilary Clinton from many other leaders in the area of loyalty was her ability to set aside her personal feelings and answer the call of duty. When she accepted the position of U.S. Secretary of State, her loyalty was not to any one person, but to country.

Loyalty is about self-sacrifice, dedication to duty, and the willingness to serve. Let us put this in a different context to get a greater understanding of this type of loyalty. How many people would compete for a high-level position, not be selected for the post, yet accept a lower-level position working for the very person they were in direct competition with? For many, their ego would get in the way of loyalty.

Let us take an even closer look at loyalty. In my two decades of working in public safety, I have learned and experienced many different types of subcultures. Some of these subcultures held questionable values. Some of these subcultures held questionable beliefs about other members in their organization. Early in my career, I learned to be loyal to the principles of my profession and not to one particular person or group. Loyalty to the profession will always ensure that the individual's ethics, integrity, character, and credibility remain intact.

A leader that is loyal to a person or organization may find themselves in the same place as the 35 educators from the Atlanta Public School system that were indicted in one of the largest public school cheating scandals in the United States. A leader that is loyal to the profession of education would have spoken out against those practices. A good leader would have realized how much the entire school district's reputation would suffer. There is a saying that "one bad apple does not spoil the whole bunch," but in the public safety and public service arena, one bad apple makes is very difficult for the whole bunch to maintain its credibility.

Remember most public safety professions take an oath of office. This oath is a commitment to adhere to the principles upon which the profession was established. This oath is not a blind commitment to the organization or the organization leader, but to the profession of public safety and what it stands for.

Enthusiastic

What type of person would you most likely follow? Would you rather follow a leader who is upbeat and focused or a leader who allows the current climate to guide their emotions? If you are enthusiastic and have a reputation for getting results, personal success will follow. On being enthusiastic, Norman Vincent Peele wrote, "Your enthusiasm will be infectious, stimulating, and impressive to others. They will love you for it. They will go for you and with you."

Leadership trait seven of the Marine Corps' 14 leadership traits is "ENTHUSIASM," which they define as "a sincere interest, and exuberance in the performance of your duties. If you are enthusiastic, you are optimistic, cheerful, and willing to accept the challenges." A leader must be sure that they remind their personnel of the important role they all play. In addition, leaders must challenge their staff on a regular basis not only to ensure their growth but also to remain focused on the mission.

A good leader should be enthusiastic. Very few cynics are real leaders even though they may have the title. Good leaders are committed to the future. If the leader harbors any doubts or negativity as to what the future holds, their team will unquestionably feel it. A leader's actions and deportment must be carried out with absolute integrity. When leaders are sincerely enthusiastic, active, energetic, and confident, they will be able to harness the energy that is already within their team to achieve success.

Accountable

This should be the shortest section of this chapter. We are all too familiar with the term *accountability*. Anyone you ask who holds a leadership position will often speak of accountability, but often he or she may hold members of his or her organization to a higher standard of accountability. A good leader must take responsibility for their actions as well as the actions of their team. A good leader will be accountable when things go wrong, and will publicly endorse their team when there are successes.

As the mayor of New York City, Rudy Giuliani demanded accountability from his personnel. We cannot deny the impact Giuliani had on reducing the crime rate in New York City. Giuliani outlined his beliefs as they pertain to leadership in his book, titled *Leadership*. This book is highly recommended for anyone who is serious about developing his or her leadership skills.

Many will say that when he was mayor, Giuliani was an autocratic or authoritative leader, but in reading his book and researching his past, you will see that he gave people in upper management positions the opportunity to succeed or fail. When they succeeded, they were rewarded, but when they failed, they were replaced. Agree or disagree, leaders at all levels must hold themselves accountable when it comes to successfully achieving the mission. To whom much is given, much will always be required!

Former New York City Mayor Rudy Giuliani made a statement in his book about leadership that I guarantee many who read the book missed. In summary, he said, "Weddings are optional, funerals are mandatory." Here is the takeaway; no one remembers all of the people that attended his or her wedding. Most of the time, couples will not know who attended their wedding until they begin the process of sending thank you cards. In contrast, a funeral is one of the most difficult times that people will experience, and if you think back to a close family member's funeral, you often remember those that attended. This statement is important because a leader should possess the desire to show compassion for the people they lead. It shows a personal level of accountability that intertwines with the professional level of accountability. The interlinking of personal and professional accountability establishes an excellent foundation on which the legacy of a leader can be built.

Former President George W. Bush authored a book titled "Decision Points." There is a section in the book in which the former president looks back at how he handled the hurricane disaster in New Orleans. The former president acknowledges that the situation could have been handled better. As the leader of the country, he took responsibility for the disaster response, although there was political infighting between the mayor and governor. Former President Bush held himself accountable, and to this day, he refuses to speak negatively about anyone that presides over the office he once held. Many leaders can learn valuable lessons from this leadership trait.

Decisive

"In any moment decisions, the best decision is the right decision; the next best decision is the wrong decision, and the worst decision is no decision." This quote reminds me of the importance of being decisive. This quote is believed to have come from former President Theodore Roosevelt. Being a leader means making decisions. Organizations should expect leaders at all levels to take action in difficult situations.

There is a myriad of methods designed to help people make good decisions, but inevitably, moment decisions are a time when the leader relies on their natural instincts. Utilizing the natural instincts to make moment decisions can be perilous, but the leader that combines their natural instincts with a sound decision-making model will turn anxious moments into moments of tranquility.

When US Airways Flight 1549 hit a flock of geese after taking off from New York's LaGuardia Airport, Pilot Chesley Sullenberger encountered a moment decision. With the 90-ton aircraft disabled and 155 passengers on board, Sullenberger had to make a decision. Everyone knows that Sullenberger successfully landed the plane on the Hudson River, but notice what separates him from many other pilots. Following the bird strike, the air traffic controller asked Flight 1549 to return to LaGuardia Airport.

I am of the belief that most pilots would have allowed the air traffic controller to make that decision for them, but Captain Sullenberger knew that was not an option. Captain Sullenberger considered an alternative airport but quickly realized that would lead to a tragic conclusion. This resulted in the decision to land the enormous plane on the Hudson River.

In describing his feelings during the troubled flight, Captain Sullenberger said, "It felt as if the bottom had fallen out of our world. I could feel my pulse and my blood pressure shoot up, my perceptual feed narrow, because of the stress. But I had the discipline to focus on the task at hand in spite of it." Despite all that was taking place around Captain Sullenberger, he managed to concentrate on the task.

Captain Sullenberger like many other great leaders made a moment decision that successfully saved the lives of everyone on board flight 1549. In any moment decision, Roosevelt's words hold true: The best decision is the right decision, the next best decision is the wrong decision, and the worst decision is no decision at all.

Being decisive does not always dictate a solo approach; there may be times when the group has to be involved. The Vroom-Jago decision model is a rational model used by leaders to determine whether they should make a decision alone or involve a group, and to what extent the group should be involved. In some business situations, it is better for a leader to be the decision maker for the group. In others, it is best for the group to have some input or even make the decision. This model distinguishes five different situations and outlines an algorithm for determining which one to use. Research the Vroom-Yago decision-making model and learn how you can best utilize the Vroom-Jago decision tree.

Ethical

Ethical issues can be one of the most stressful situations a leader will encounter. I have firsthand experience interacting with leaders who glossed over unethical conduct. They were more concerned with the reputation of their agency. What they did not understand was that their behavior was even more destructive than the conduct they minimized. Minimizing unethical conduct is one of the quickest ways for a leader to lose their credibility amongst followers. Followers carefully watch how leaders respond to unethical behavior and conduct. When leaders fail to respond to unethical behavior in a transparent and firm manner, members of their organization lose respect.

Jerald Greenberg developed the theory of Organizational Justice. This is a theory that focuses on how members of an organization perceive fairness and impartial treatment. In summary, when members of organizations perceive that they are treated unfairly, it affects employee turnover, job satisfaction, organizational commitment, task execution, and trust.

One of the quickest ways for a leader to lose credibility is to demand ethical conduct from their subordinates, but fail to speak out when their peers, or their boss, exhibit conduct that may be considered unethical. There are tactful ways to address ethical issues, without making people feel as though it is the end of their world.

When encountering members of an agency that may have exhibited unethical conduct, a leader should approach the situation in this manner: Listen, Evaluate, Assess, Decide, Engage, and Resolve (L.E.A.D.E.R). Sometimes you have to step back and look at a situation from all angles. What may appear unethical to one person may be ethical to others. Step back, listen, and then look at it from a wide-angle lens. Evaluate the impact of the situation or condition. Assess the people involved to determine their level of training and position within the organization. Why is this important? Obviously, if the personnel involved are senior members of the organization, then they should be aware of the values of the organization. Decide on a course of action. Do not delay, the more you delay, the more likely you will be pulled into an ethical quagmire. Engage the parties involved. This means helping members of the organization learn from the situation. To disengage would be to miss out on an excellent teaching opportunity. Finally, there should be a resolution in which every person involved understands that something did occur, and discuss why it amounted to a critical level or not. Close out the situation, do not let it fester or try to bury it alive because it will come back to haunt you and the entire organization.

In his autobiography titled "My American Journey," Colin Powell takes the reader on a ride through the peaks and valleys of his journey to becoming the National Security Advisor for the late former President Ronald Reagan. From the onset of the journey, Powell never compromises his integrity, credibility, or character; this is why many believe he resigned from the Secretary of State position after it was determined, that Iraq may not have possessed weapons of mass destruction (WMD). That subject is still being debated by political commentators and in the annals of some lecture halls around the world.

In the end, Colin Powell is and always will be a great American hero because of his rise through the ranks of the military and his work while serving in cabinet positions under former Presidents George H.W. Bush and George W. Bush. Finally, Colin Powell is a great American hero, because of his commitment to maintaining the highest ethical standards.

Resourceful

Deloitte Touche Tohmatsu Limited is the largest professional services network in the world, based on revenue and the more than 200,000 professionals that are employed in some capacity for the company. Deloitte identified eight core behaviors of resourceful leaders. These eight behaviors are; openness to possibilities, the ability to collaborate, demonstration of belief in their team and people, personal resilience and tenacity, the ability to create and sustain commitment across the system, display of a focus on results and outcomes, the ability to simplify, and the ability to learn continuously. Now go back and slowly read Deloitte's eight core behaviors and compare your resourcefulness with that of Deloitte.

Robert Needham, in his book *Team Secrets of the Navy SEALS: The Elite Military Force's Leadership Principles for Business,"* said that by treating members of your organization with respect and remaining cognizant of their needs, they will become a satisfied and fulfilled entity. In addition, Needham said leaders should take the time to find out who is working for them. I had a squadron commander that knew the names of every personnel that was under his command. Even though a leader will have to ask individual members or their organization to sacrifice for the common good, they must always remember that each member is human and has individual needs that must be met for them to be a useful part of their organization. If you project Mr. Needham's views, then in all likelihood you will exhibit the core behaviors listed by Deloitte.

Being resourceful is the art of being high-spirited no matter the situation or the circumstances. That is what people look for in a leader, especially when the odds are against them. Followers look for someone who has the best interest of the entire team at heart, without putting the mission at risk. Being resourceful is not just about obtaining resources or equipment; it is about speaking to the hearts and minds of people while at the same time successfully achieving the task.

The Fundamentals of being a C.O.A.C.H

"Average leaders raise the bar on themselves; good leaders raise the bar for others; great leaders inspire others to raise their own bar."
Orrin Woodward

When you leave, what will your legacy be? How many future leaders will you have developed? How many people will you have touched in your career?

Several college and professional athletic coaches have published books on leadership. Maybe it is time for a leader to speak on the topic of coaching. Coaches have an inordinate amount of influence over their players. Think about this; a coach can make or break a player by the way they develop them. Have you ever watched a person play out of position or operate in an area in which they were unable to utilize their strengths? What that means is they are working in an area that is not affording them the opportunity to maximize their abilities or skill sets.

Have you ever witnessed a person struggle in a position that they were ill equipped to handle? This means the person is being set up for failure. As a leader, you should have a desire to coach people, to develop them so they reach their maximum potential. This will require the ability to discern your follower's weakness and strengths, which means, you will have to spend time with your followers. Is that not what a coach is required to do? One of the easiest and most effective ways a leader can develop the tools to be a good coach is by remembering the acronym C.O.A.C.H. This acronym stands for Consistency, Opportunity, Assertiveness, Competency, and Honesty. Let us look at each of these terms as they apply to leadership.

Consistency

People can be consistently bad or consistently good, or as the Christian Bible says, in summary, people can be hot or cold, but a lukewarm person is worth nothing. A good leader will be consistent in attitude, character, and authority. The worse thing that can happen to a leader is to be compared to Forrest Gump's box of chocolates. Tom Hanks, who plays the character Forrest Gump, speaks this favorite line while seated at a bus stop, chatting to a woman, "Mama always said life was like a box of chocolates. You never know what you're gonna get."

The worse type of leader is the one from whom you never know what you are going to get, from one day to the next. They are hot one day and cold the next, which in essence, makes them lukewarm. Think about this: lukewarm is good for nothing. Try drinking a glass of lukewarm soda, or try soaking in lukewarm water.

A leader should always strive to be consistent in their demeanor, in the way they treat others because consistency will enable the leader to build a rapport with people in and out of the organization. How often have you encountered someone in a leadership role that on occasion would come into the workplace in a bad mood? These types of people will kill the morale of the entire office in a fraction of a second. What makes these kinds of leaders even worse is when they come in the next day, upbeat and ready to save the world. What do you think the followers of these types of leaders think of them? How often are the coworkers on edge when that person enters the door? A good leader does not wake up on the wrong side of the bed; the good leader chooses to wake up on the right side of the bed every day!

Consistency is not to be confused with stagnation or the status quo; being consistent is being levelheaded and even-handed in your dealings with people. Subordinates often look for opportunities to exploit management's inconsistencies, especially in how they treat their people, or how they respond to situations. The fastest way for a leader to lose credibility is to be horribly inconsistent when exercising their authority. Misuse and abuse of power can cause significant harm to people and create a sense of cynicism and mistrust in failed authority (Burke et al., 2006).

How does a leader focus on being consistent? Since we are using the acronym C.O.A.C.H., then we should think about a coach's preparation. Coaches love practicing as much as they love playing the game. Coaches know that in practice is where the learning takes place because practice leads to consistency. Practice being consistent when interacting with everyone at all levels in your organization. Greet everyone in the same manner, discipline in a consistent manner, and do not allow yourself to be part of the gossip line no matter how enticing it may be. Even when the leader is not feeling well, they have to maintain a level of consistency. The old cliché is that you practice the way you play. If you do not practice consistency, then you will never be consistent; thus, people will be hesitant to trust you.

Openness

Openness is akin to transparency, and many leaders in public safety have a difficult time with transparency. The reason behind this is very straightforward. Some people have to hold onto all of the information, and they are afraid to be completely open with subordinates and peers for fear of losing power or exposing a weakness. Openness is important because it promotes teamwork and contributes to the organization's lines of communications remaining open.

Once someone withholds information, it creates a lack of mistrust and brings into question the leader's motives. Openness enables the manager to create a shared vision in which everyone can see where the leader and the organization are trying to go. Senge (2006) adds that the ability of leaders to hold a shared picture of the future they seek to create has inspired organizations for thousands of years. In contrast, he states that many leaders have personal visions that never are translated into shared visions that would galvanize an organization.

In summary, the openness of a leader not only builds trust, but it instills confidence in their followers and inspires them to work for the betterment of the team and the organization. A leader who fails to be transparent will soon find that their team is not on the same page or even in the same book. A leader that fails to be transparent will experience a significant disconnect from their personnel and the community they serve.

One of the biggest hindrances to openness is today's technology. The new forms of leader-follower communication consist of emails, intranet, and text messaging. It can be disastrous when a leader communicates to their peers and subordinates primarily through technology, especially when the leader is in the same locale as their followers. I have witnessed many email wars amongst management that entangled subordinates, peers, and upper-level management, simply because someone was unable to utilize their verbal skills effectively enough to convey their displeasure with someone or a situation.

Openness is allowing followers to be actively engaged with their leader, and it is important for followers to receive verbal feedback and guidance from their leaders. Openness is critical to coaching and is one of the main keys to the development of personnel.

Openness builds trust and confidence throughout the organization. Most leaders expect their followers to be open, but some leaders will not be forthright in their communication with those same followers. Openness is about open communication from the lowest level to the highest, and then back down to the lowest. It does not involve the filtering of information as it travels up and down the various levels of the organization. This creates issues for many organizations because the filtering of information leaves each level with only limited knowledge, which in turn causes the decision makers to be uninformed. This can be devastating and potentially costly to many organizations.

In the public safety field, openness enhances the organization's reputation with the public. I often wonder why so many organizational leaders rebuke public assistance in the form of citizen's review boards or other citizen panels. In corporate America, the investors monitor how an organization is run. The customers monitor the quality of the services being provided.

In public safety, the investors (tax paying citizens) and the customers (citizens) rarely have any input into how the organization serves them. This is due in part to tradition and the subculture of some public safety agencies. A leader gains the trust of persons inside and outside of the organization through open communication and transparency.

Assertiveness

If you are a leader, you must be actively involved in developing your personnel. A coach is a hands-on leader that actively engages their inner and outer environment. They seek various methods to teach and learn, often through a commonsense approach. It is like the cheeseburger illustration in the "Transforming Leadership" section: this image exhibits how often in life; we use visionary methods to make a point.

Being assertive is to be a great communicator through active listening skills. Assertive leaders understand that the art of listening is more important than speaking. General George C. Marshall once stated, "Passive inactivity, because you have not been given specific instructions to do this or do that, is a serious deficiency." In essence, just because you have not been told to do something does not mean you do nothing. Assertiveness means to focus continually on better ways to enhance systems, personnel, and entire organizations; this may not be the favored approach, but the assertive leader understands systems organizations, behaviors of groups, and what is needed to create impactful change in their respective organizations.

Competency

The competency portion of this section is in many ways the foundation of coaching. People are willing to learn from those who have immersed themselves in becoming an expert or specialist. Coaching someone is depositing knowledge and wisdom into their cognitive bank account. An astute coach will seek ways to increase their knowledge while at the same time transferring that knowledge to their subordinates and peers.

Let us take a moment to reflect on the term *competency*. Many people have different views on what makes a person competent, but the bottom line is the leader-coach is proficient and capable. They are the leaders that know that their success comes from the success of their followers. Imagine seeing the subordinates and peers that you coached exceeding their limitations and expectations.

The competent coach will have a strong desire for continued learning. I know of many coaches that never won a championship, but many of their assistants obtained head positions and won numerous titles. A competent leader will develop a multitude of people because they have a passion for learning and teaching.

John Maxwell said, "Competence goes beyond words. It is the leader's ability to say it, plan it, and do it in such a way that others know that you know how and know that they want to follow you." Leaders must believe in themselves, in the people they lead, and in what they are trying to do. Leadership at the Ford Motor Company peaked my interest, when they refused to accept the second round of government-infused funding to continue production. I wanted to know whom the CEO was during the 2008 economic meltdown. Alan Mulally was the name that surfaced on Internet search engines. A book that I highly recommend is, "American Icon: Alan Mulally and the Fight to save Ford," written by Bryce Hoffman. This book shows how a competent leader successfully and efficiently accomplishes their goals.

Alan Mulally transforms the culture of a tradition-laden, self-serving organization into an accountable, resourceful, and contemporary company that put its customers first. If Alan Mulally can do that at Ford, surely leaders in public safety can transform the culture, but it takes expertise and proficiency in many areas to accomplish this. This can be accomplished by placing people around you that strengthen your weaknesses and compliment your strengths. What if you were the CEO of GM or Chrysler, and you learned that Ford was not accepting government funding?

One final thought on competency comes from one of my personal experiences. Throughout this text, I have tried to keep my own experiences to a minimum because it is more important to learn from other people's successes and mistakes, so we repeat the successes and not the mistakes. I encountered a person in a high-ranking position who had no knowledge of my team's responsibilities; in fact, he was very disinterested. What I gleaned from this experience was that he simply did not care professionally or personally.

Now ponder these two assumptions for a brief moment. Would you rather be viewed as a leader that does not care about their subordinates or a leader that has no knowledge of what their subordinates are tasked with accomplishing? If your answer was neither then you understand the importance of competency as it relates to leadership. A coach cares about what their people are doing, how they are doing it, and how they can help them accomplish it. If you are not doing any of those things, then you are just taking up space.

Honesty

Are you a trustworthy and reliable leader? If so, conduct a survey of your subordinates and see what their opinions are. If you are not concerned with what they think, then you are not seeking ways to inspire and motivate your people. Most leaders have to conduct a self-assessment before they can gain the trust of their people. Can everyone depend on you or is there only a select few that can depend on you? Are you trustworthy only to those in your inner circle, or do the majority of members in your organization see you as trustworthy, reliable, and credible?

What experiences and skill sets are necessary to build trust amongst members of your organization? Honesty is about credibility, and in the end, all we have is our credibility. Once a member of a public safety agency loses their credibility, it not only affects that person, but it affects the organization and their family. This is exacerbated when a leader of a public safety organization loses their credibility. The entire organization suffers because of the lack of trust between the agency and the general public. There have been multiple cases of corruption involving public safety agencies, which can be attributed to one individual.

Any corruption may cause a public safety agency to become disenfranchised with the community they serve. Honesty is about morality and fairness at all levels of the organization. A good leader seeks ways to ensure that all aspects of the organization that is under their control are functioning in a fair and equitable manner. Lawsuits and federal oversight can be avoided if the leadership in organizations will take the time to build trust and commitment, especially amongst members of underrepresented groups.

Be honest about what your goals and visions are. Be honest about the state of your agency. Many leaders often publicly stress that their agency is the best in the country, but if that is an honest assessment, then why have a vision. A vision statement paints a picture of what an organization seeks to achieve or accomplish. If your organization is the best, then what is left to achieve? If you are the best, then what else can you learn? Be honest in pointing out deficiencies and weaknesses, and then begin strengthening those areas, whether they are your weaknesses, your subordinates' weaknesses, or weaknesses in your organization.

Diversity: Building Better Internal and External Relationships

"Remember, teamwork begins by building trust. And the only way to do that is to overcome our need for invulnerability."
Patrick Lencioni

A search of the Internet reveals the difficulties public safety organizations have with diversity hiring. Most subheadings in the articles show that there is a perception that there are not enough qualified women and racial minorities available for hire. In addition, public safety agencies claim that the women and racial minorities that may be qualified are being employed by corporate America.

To publicly state that there are not enough qualified women is stating that there are not enough competent or able-bodied woman, or that women from the local community are unfit to do the job. Those agencies are publicly stating that women and racial minorities in their communities are incapable of satisfying the requirements to become a police officer or firefighter.

In addition, when an organization publicly states that they cannot recruit and hire qualified women and racial minorities, employees associated with that organization might place members of those underrepresented groups in a generalized category. Employees within the organization may not seek to recruit women and racial minorities because they have been told they are "not qualified." Women and racial minority community members may not seek employment with the organization because they feel as though they will not have a fair chance or an equal opportunity because the agency has placed them in a generalized category of being unqualified.

When situations like these occur, the members of the majority in that organization can take on an elitist attitude because they have been categorized by their agency as being the "most qualified." Finally, once a woman or racial minority is hired, members of the majority might perceive that there was an exception made or handout given to that particular individual or group. How will the woman or racial minority cadet excel in the training academy or out in the field? Do those public statements lead to greater racial and gender conflict within the organization? Do those public statements feed into public safety culture and add to the marginalization of women and racial minority police officers?

Bolton (2003) examined the workplace experiences of African American police officers and found that there is a shared perception amongst them that systematic barriers exist in agencies that limit their advancement and affect career longevity. African American officers reported a lack of support networks and constant conflict and stress. Moreover, many of those interviewed explained that they were exposed to racial jokes, cartoons, name-calling, slurs, rudeness, and petty harassment.

Research shows that gay, lesbian, and bisexual officers who choose to remain "closeted" do so out of fear of reprisal, fear of rejection, offensive jokes, pranks, and overt harassment and discrimination (Buhrke, 1996). Finally, studies also reveal that women police officers are more likely than male officers to encounter higher levels of overt hostility and other negative social interactions on the job, including negative attitudes of male officers, exposure to tragedy and trouble, group blame and rumors, exposure to profanity and sex jokes, and stigmatization due to appearance (Brandl & Hassell, 2009).

A search of the U.S. Department of Justice website reveals how these issues affect public safety organizations in the form of lawsuits and consent decrees. Any environment that is perceived to be hostile is not the culture a public safety executive should be proud to lead. If discriminatory or harassing attitudes have permeated throughout the public safety culture, then one should question the type of treatment members of the community are receiving from those that expose their peers to racial jokes, slurs, and harassment.

Finally, what treatment do women in the community receive from police officers that expose their female counterparts to rumors, profanity, and sexually charged jokes? To say women and racial minorities are not qualified sends a message that the behaviors described in this paragraph are organizationally acceptable.

Leadership and Diversity

Why is the topic of diversity in a book about leadership? We currently live in a global society. Society has changed drastically over the past few decades. Ask any person who has recently been interviewed for an executive or upper-level management position, and they will tell you that diversity was a topic of discussion. The term diversity has created a firestorm in the bowels of the public safety arena. An astute leader will perceive whether the majority of their members have a positive or negative attitude toward diversity.

Why do many members of public safety organizations avoid the topic of diversity? There may be many answers to this question. It boils down to the agency's failure to implement an all-inclusive diversity training program. Many purported diversity training programs alienate the majority. If the majority of the members of an organization are not receptive to diversity training, how will they ever be receptive to the diversity initiatives of their leader?

Diversity training should focus on a multicultural, inclusive approach that does not marginalize any group, and does not seek to completely eradicate individual biases from their members. At one time Sir Robert Peel, the father of modern policing, was biased toward

Catholics. Even August Vollmer, the acclaimed community-policing guru, was purported to be sympathetic toward the Nazi movement. Any training that any individual perceives as an attempt to change their worldview will be met with extreme resistance. Philosophically, the goal should be to help individuals recognize their biases and to develop methods to enable them to work through those biases.

Diversity training has received negative attention because most of the time it has been taught in an adversarial manner. Diversity training should not be divisive, accusatory, or surface based, but should stress the importance of past, present, and future contributions of all groups, to include the majority group. Diversity training must focus on enhancing communication amongst various groups to include generations.

Many lawsuits have been a result of verbal communication or acts that were guided by the individual's biases. A portion of diversity training should be attributed to the management of personal biases, as well as the personal and organizational liabilities associated with unmanaged personal biases.

What every public safety leader should understand is that their organization is one of few where all of their customers are also their owners and investors. Without the support of the customers and the external stakeholders, an organization will consistently falter and ultimately fall under federal oversight (consent decree). Every organization should embrace diversity and see it as an opportunity instead of an alternative term for affirmative action. Questions we must ask ourselves is not why we should seek diversity, but ask those that are questioning the need for diversity to explain why an organization should not seek diversity.

Development—Growth and Change

Diversity allows for growth and expansion in the organization. This growth happens from an individual and collective perspective. Diversity causes personnel to develop an open mind to various cultures and backgrounds. Diversity creates change in an organization that is reflective of the changes that occur in our societies. A diverse agency enables the organization to amass various methods of problem-solving, which involves utilizing personnel from different genders, race, background, culture, and even religious affiliation.

Diversity does not change the core values, mission, and vision of an organization; diversity will support and enhance the mission, vision, and purpose of an organization. Diversity assists in the agency's development of its personnel and creates a greater understanding of how to respond to customer service issues.

Innovation—Advancement, Modernization, and Improvement

We often hear the term *global society*. This is not a façade or an attempt to shove diversity down the proverbial throats of organizations. The demographics of society have changed over the past few decades. Diversity advances the organization's ability to think outside of its cultural box. It enables the organization to become a learning organization, learning different methods, strategies, and techniques to respond to situations.

With the diverse generational groups in the workplace, the importance of diversity is at an all time high. Tradition is clashing with nontraditional, the old style of policing (kick ass and take names) is battling the new school style of verbal judo, and these are all issues that affect diversity and multiculturalism. Some perceive political correctness as a softening of values, while others see it as a means to give a voice to those that have been disregarded and treated unfairly.

Yukl (2010) suggests that globalization and changing demographic patterns are making it more important for leaders to understand how to influence and manage people with different values, beliefs, and expectations. A blend of generations, cultures, and ethnicities can only enhance the ability of a public safety agency to respond to the needs of a global society.

Vitality—Strength and Vigor

Diversity of thought injects energy into a team. Imagine being in a meeting and every attendee is quietly nodding in agreement with the leadership. In addition, not one person offers an alternative thought or idea. The results of that meeting will be of no benefit to members of the organization.

Diversity entails the ability to bring various philosophies, opinions, and ideas to the table. Many times, the differing philosophies make the difference between failure and success. Every person has a worldview, and when factoring in people of various cultures, race, gender, sexual identities, and ethnicities, it creates a vast amount of knowledge.

Imagine attending a meeting to determine a method to deliver a service to a diverse group of people. If everyone at the meeting were of the same race, gender, and cultural background, it is possible the service would be advantageous to one particular group while placing underrepresented groups that were not present at a disadvantage.

Many corporations have failed in their efforts to introduce products into various communities, only because they failed to gather input from members of that particular community. Instead of strengthening ties to the community, they offended members of the community. Diversity helps to build a strong relationship, and good leadership builds sustainable community partnerships.

Education—Learning and Culture

Organizations are filled with individuals who introduce their own value preferences into the organization. These values represent the way people select actions, evaluate people and events, and explain their actions and evaluations. These value preferences shape organizational culture to a certain extent (Dauber et al., 2012).

In addition, Yukl (2010) notes that in cultures with strong "masculine" values like toughness and assertiveness, "feminine" attributes such as compassion, empathy, and intuition are not viewed as essential for effective leadership. The arena of public safety is male dominated; therefore, many of the formal and informal values that are present in the organization may be from a male perspective. The formal and informal values shape the culture of the public safety agency.

A multicultural public safety agency creates a culture of inclusivity. Personal mastery is one of the best attributes diversity brings to an organization. *Personal mastery* is a term that Peter Senge uses to describe the continual process of learning by an organization. Many public safety agencies may not engage in a continual learning process; therefore, the organization lacks the nature of a learning organization (Senge, 2006). The benefits of instituting a continual learning process may be a foreign concept in some organizations. These organizations may experience major setbacks via litigation if they neglect the concept of continuous learning.

Many public safety agencies would perceive continual learning as a weakness because it involves being aware of areas of ignorance, incompetence, and lack of growth (Senge, 2006). A leader should try accepting the fact that they may be ignorant or incompetent in some areas because it is nearly impossible to be experienced and skilled in all fields.

Learning the benefits of diversity and working to create a culture that is receptive to diversity is an indicator of one's commitment to continual learning.

Respect—Reverence and Admiration

An inclusive public safety culture breeds reverence for the differences amongst ideas and philosophies that are prevalent within the agency. Inclusivity inspires admiration for the various worldviews and value systems that contribute to the credibility of the organization in the eyes of every member of the community the organization serves. Diversity in the public safety arena is simply mutual respect for the views and cultures of everyone in the organization, and not just a select few. Diversity becomes disrespectful, when the focus remains on one or two groups, as opposed to the organization as a whole. Diversity cannot outweigh the importance of every member feeling as if they are an integral part of the team.

The leader that implements diversity measures must be aware of the need for respect on all sides of the diversity spectrum. Consider how disrespectful it is to maintain that people of a certain gender or race are not qualified to work in a particular career field. Consider how disrespectful it is when diversity is such a hot topic that the majority members are marginalized for the sake of diversity. The astute leader develops a knack for establishing a culture that is respectful of all members of the organization.

Strategic—Deliberate and Planned

Diversity is not an unplanned act on management's part. It is not something that a leader should be forced to accomplish. Diversity is not lip service or a half-hearted attempt to satisfy the media or members of the community. Diversity is a deliberate attempt at establishing an agency that represents all members of the organization and the community.

Developing a plan to create an inclusive organizational atmosphere does not happen by chance in the public safety arena. It should be part of every organization's strategic plan because it involves members of the organization as well as members of the community.

If an agency receives grants from the federal government, then it more than likely has an Equal Employment Opportunity Plan (EEOP). This plan establishes a method of recruiting individuals from underrepresented groups. If an agency is nationally accredited then it more than likely has met standards established by the accrediting organization on recruitment and selection methods. EEOPs provide a foundation for recruitment and hiring, and these plans should be communicated to all members of the organization.

Elite—Leading and Influential

Multicultural Inclusion (MCI) is a way to implement and train in matters of diversity without alienating others. MCI is not a new form of diversity training, but it is the best way to learn and teach diversity without creating a divisive environment. Multicultural Inclusion will help to break down the resistance to the term *diversity* because it stresses the importance of everyone's culture. For example, if you consider two individuals, regardless of race or gender, one from the West Coast and one from the East Coast, it would be easy to understand how these two people could have different societal views as well as values. Even though individuals may have differing ideas on how to handle an issue, it is important to hear both of their viewpoints.

Socioeconomic status (SES) is an area that is largely neglected when diversity is the topic of discussion. What would happen if we suddenly placed an individual from lower socioeconomic background amongst a group of people with a higher socioeconomic background? While the person with lower SES may not have many things in common with the individuals from higher SES, both groups can still learn from each other if they have an open mind. In contrast, if the group of higher SES individuals feels as though the person with lower SES received a subpar education, how much would they be willing to learn from that individual? Socioeconomics plays a significant role in how people are perceived. I have witnessed the affect a persons SES can have on their recruitment and hiring. Because an individual from lower SES may have been exposed to various negative situations as a youth, they face a higher chance of being eliminated during the public safety hiring process. Unfortunately, individuals from lower SES will often have a successful career in public safety if give the opportunity because their experience affords them the ability to engage people at all levels.

The leader that cares about all-inclusiveness will ensure that all members of the organization feel as though they are valuable assets to the organization. These leaders will make sure the organization promotes the value of diversity in a holistic manner. Leading various cultures requires the leader to be culturally competent, collaborative, and compassionate. In addition, other common themes of effective leadership across varying cultures are the leader's ability to articulate a tangible vision and to be a facilitator for cultural change.

The Curse of Marginalization

Finally, leaders of public safety organizations that seek to build better relations with the various cultures in their communities must ensure that all members of their organization receive diversity and leadership development training. Marginalization occurs when leaders appoint members of their organization to interact with segments of the community that share the same race, ethnicity, and gender. When something occurs in an ethnic community, why do leaders assume that an officer that shares the same ethnicity is better suited to address the situation? A great leader will ensure that any member of their organization possesses the ability to build and rebuild community relationships.

In public safety agencies, there are personnel of various races and ethnicities that can interact with different segments of the community. Unfortunately, when a leader selects individuals that share the same physical characteristics as members of the community, it shows that the organization has not embraced the concept of diversity.

Every leader should be aware of the history of their profession. If a leader of a police department has an awareness of the history of policing, they will understand that many minority officers were hired just to work in the minority communities. Many leaders thought that placing minority officers in the minority communities would create a better relationship between that particular community and the police department. This thought process created division within the police department and had very little effect on police-community relations.

An astute leader will have confidence that all members of their organization will have the capacity to address concerns from members of the community. We all have different worldviews and come from various backgrounds, so even if we share the same physical features, that is not an indicator that we will share the same views. If all personnel have a general understanding of the various cultures that they interact with on a daily basis, any member of an organization should be able to communicate effectively with the community. In public safety, 90 percent of the time is spent communicating with citizens.

Do not marginalize members of the community and members of your organization by engaging in this practice. At the end of the day, if it is a crisis that is dividing the organization and the community, the community will see every member of the organization as being a part of the problem, regardless of their race, ethnicity, and gender. When community relations are being impacted, the leader has to step up and lead.

Organization-wide leadership training will enhance the agency's community relations. Diversity training can only go so far, but leadership training builds an organization of people who are equipped to handle every situation. Lastly, invite every community leader, business owner, local politician, and other community groups to the table to help build better relationships.

Dismantling the Wall of Silence

"The ultimate measure of a man is not where he stands in moments of comfort, but where he stands at times of challenge and controversy." Martin Luther King, Jr.

I cannot count the number of times I have heard people in public safety organizations say, "We do not want our dirty laundry aired!" This quote should be especially troubling to leaders that operate in the field of public safety and public service. Statements like these contribute to the fortification of the wall of silence.

Leaders should be transparent and willing to show the community that they are cleaning the dirty laundry, and if it cannot be cleaned, then the dirty laundry has to be thrown out. Every organization has internal issues, and for any public safety manager to lack the fortitude to speak out about those issues goes against every leadership theory that has ever been researched. Leaders are quick to defend the actions of their personnel and should be just as quick to condemn any actions taken by their staff that affects public trust.

In 2012, a federal judge found that the Chicago Police Department's Internal Affairs Bureau purposely suppressed investigations of misconduct (Farber, 2013). The federal judge identified the Chicago Police Department's flawed investigative process as being guided by the blue wall of silence. The *blue wall of silence* is unwillingness by police department employees to report misconduct on the part of a fellow employee. In a time when police and community relations are at their lowest point since before September 11, 2001, each public safety leader has to assess the culture of their organization.

An examination of statistics on the Internal Affairs division of various organizations has revealed some interesting numbers. For example, external complaints against police officers were sustained 10–20% of the time while internal complaints initiated by superiors were sustained nearly 90% of the time. These statistics reveal that these particular agencies may adhere to the blue wall of silence by silencing the external complaints and framing the internal complaints to a pre-conceived disposition.

There was an occasion when a group of university students along with members of the community marched to the headquarters of the local police department. The marchers were trying to deliver a message protesting recent cases of police brutality. In addition, the group demanded a change in the way the police department conducted its policing methods. Nearly a month later, police officers from that police department sprayed several of the university's students with pepper spray. This incident occurred after celebrations got out of control following a high-profile sporting event. In a news conference the following day, the police chief justified the police officers' use of pepper spray, but a few hours later launched an internal investigation. The internal investigation was initiated after photographs were presented to the chief showing students and members of the news media being pepper sprayed while standing on a sidewalk.

The leader of this agency, whether intentionally or unintentionally, reinforced the blue wall of silence. In this case, the chief may have fortified the blue wall of silence by initially justifying the actions of the police officers before having all of the facts. Because citizens throughout the United States perceive that there is a culture of silence permeating police departments, the leader's actions may have reinforced this perception (Dempsey & Forst, 2010).

The perception of the culture of silence puts additional strain on police and community relations. Leaders should refrain from speaking out about sensitive cases until all of the facts are known. This will help the leader to remain unbiased and impartial, which is what public safety personnel took an oath to do.

The wall of silence is not unique to public safety organizations. The wall of silence exists in many public safety agencies and often builds to a fever pitch because of the politics involved in leading these organizations. A transparent leader will continually build the trust of the public, but a leader who is unwilling to be translucent will quickly lose the confidence of the public. Once the trust of the public is lost, it will take several years to rebuild that confidence.

Public safety agencies across the United States have expressed the need for change because of the increased tension between their organizations and members of the community. In a study on organizational change, Quinn and Weick (1999) noted that organizations feel the need to orchestrate change when they encounter problems. In this case, the public safety agencies must seek change or else they may find themselves fighting against the very people that they took an oath to serve.

Leaders of public safety organizations must realize that their organizations are in a unique situation. Public safety is one of the few entities in which their customers are also their owners and investors. It is only by taxpayer monies that most public safety entities can exist, and it is through these taxpayer dollars that public safety personnel receive their salaries.

Changing the culture of an organization involves people. The way to involve people is to follow the P.E.O.P.L.E principle of change.

Planning and Implementation

The first step in planning and implementation is to determine the positive and negative effects on the organization if it changes, or if it decides not to change. This step should involve the Organizational Culture Assessment Instrument (OCAI) results along with open discussion by all stakeholders. An additional purpose of this step is to ensure members of the organization understand that there are things that will not change, and there are items that need to change. Studies have provided evidence that a sense of urgency should be the first step in implementing change (Kotter, 1995). Those studies also identify a sense of importance as being significant in implementing change (Kotter, 1995). Unfortunately, a sense of urgency may lead to strong resistance from members of the organization, but instilling a sense of importance may build a collaboration of commitment. This first step requires all members of the organization to rationalize the need for change, as well as the need to maintain the status quo in particular areas of the organization.

The second step in the process should be the development of initiatives. These initiatives are strategic in nature and involve identifying the functions of the organization that should be terminated, initiated, or improved. For example, most police departments promote their police training academies as quasi-military environments. The quasi-military philosophy is an outdated practice that should be undone because the cadets are not preparing for a war or even a quasi-war for that matter. In contrast, the police cadets are being trained to keep the peace. A semi-military training environment for police officers may fuel the "us against them" mentality and might reinforce the blue wall of silence.

The third step in the plan should be to identify areas and programs in the organization that demonstrate the core values that will characterize its preferred future cultural profile. This step will enable the organization to publicly narrate events that capture the essence of what the new organizational culture will resemble. For example, public recognition of employees that have made a difference in police-community relations should be made public. Many police officers may volunteer as youth coaches, mentors, and in many other capacities, and they too should be recognized. The efforts of the officer's volunteer efforts should be continuously promoted. Additionally, officers that volunteer in the community should not be an anomaly but should be an ordinary occurrence.

Public safety agencies should sponsor community appreciation festivals. These festivals enable the organizations to connect with the community by displaying vehicles and equipment. A festival allows for the dissemination of information and creates an excellent recruitment atmosphere. How often does a public safety agency sponsor a public event, in which it pays for the food and entertainment? Imagine an annual event in which all members of the community look forward to attending and interacting with their public safety officials.

Establishing Goals

One of the keys to success is to change the way an organization functions (Beer, Eisenstat, & Spector, 1990). The key is to transform the culture of the organization by changing the behavior of its employees. The goal of any cultural change project in law enforcement is to develop a comprehensive plan that will begin the process of dismantling the blue wall of silence. Disassembling the wall of silence requires a change process that should focus on transforming the police culture.

The blue wall of silence has been a part of the police culture since policing began in the 1800s (Dempsey & Forst, 2010). Therefore, the undoing of this metaphoric wall will require a long-term commitment, trust, and patience. In addition, the plan has to be flexible enough to adapt to an oft-changing society.

Organizational Readiness/Stakeholder Analysis

Before the development of a strategy for change, members of the organization should have an understanding of the problem the organization is confronting (Beer, Eisenstat, & Spector, 1990). The use of tools such as the OCAI can assess an organization's readiness for change.

The OCAI also assists the assessor in gaining insight into the attitudes of the stakeholders, as well as determining an outlook for the future of the agency. Multiple studies have revealed a connection between an organization's culture and the way the organization performs (Cameron & Quinn, 2011).

Leaders of law enforcement organizations should seek methods to gauge their organization's culture in comparison to how the organization interacts with the community. In addition, to lessen the likelihood of employee resistance, the leaders must be perceptive and sensitive to the needs of their personnel (Falkenberg, Haueng, Meyer, & Stensaker, 2002).

For organizational change to be successful, the agency must outline an occupational problem that will enable them to develop a successful plan for change (Beer, Eisenstat, & Spector, 1990). In this particular instance, the occupational problem is the relationship between police and community.

Promoting and Marketing

Communication is an essential step in implementing change in a public safety organization. While the fourth stage may be considered the most important, it is essential to understand that transparent communication should be ongoing. The importance of communication has been established throughout the summary of the previous section. It is a known fact the there will be resistance to cultural change in organizations. It is in the change process that employees are not just confronted with changes in their professional lives, but they may also be challenged with adapting to changes in their personal lives.

With the influence of the labor unions, the change in culture is likely to receive substantial resistance. For reasons given above, effectively communicating the culture shift is a vital component in overcoming resistance and building commitment.

Promoting and marketing also involves building an emotional and rational case for change by spreading a message of revitalization to all organizational departments (Beer, Eisenstat, & Spector, 1990). Another component of this step is the involvement of middle managers in the communication process, which will ensure that the message of revitalization does not come solely from the top of the organization, but also from the middle levels (Beer, Eisenstat, & Spector, 1990).

There has to be a particular message to build consensus to the change effort (Armenakis, Field, & Harris, 1999). The change message has to create certain core sentiments in members of the organization. The change message should be marketed and promoted in a manner that builds trust amongst the members of the organization. Once members develop trust in the concept of change, individually and organizationally, it increases the likelihood of success (Armenakis, Field, & Harris, 1999). An organization that wants to change the behavior of its personnel has to assess how it communicates the message to its employees.

The organization's mission statement should be posted on every floor of its building in big, bold letters. Each division or bureau that has its own mission statement should have it posted in the main areas of their offices.

Finally, a crucial step to creating lasting change in an organization is to include a leadership development program specifically designed for entry-level employees and frontline supervisors. This program should focus on fundamental principles that outline the leader's concept of the values members of the organization will represent. For example, in a law enforcement organization, the nine principles of policing that were developed by Sir Robert Peel is an excellent source for developing leaders in an organization.

Sir Robert Peel, considered the "father of policing," developed the law enforcement model that is still prevalent today. His principles are as follows:

PRINCIPLE 1 "The basic mission for which the police exist is to prevent crime and disorder."

PRINCIPLE 2 "The ability of the police to perform their duties is dependent upon public approval of police actions."

PRINCIPLE 3 "Police must secure the willing cooperation of the public in voluntary observance of the law to be able to secure and maintain the respect of the public."

PRINCIPLE 4 "The degree of cooperation of the public that can be secured diminishes proportionately to the necessity of the use of physical force."

PRINCIPLE 5 "Police seek and preserve public favor not by catering to the public opinion but by constantly demonstrating absolute impartial service to the law."

PRINCIPLE 6 "Police use physical force to the extent necessary to secure observance of the law or to restore order only when the exercise of persuasion, advice, and warning is found to be insufficient."

PRINCIPLE 7 "Police, at all times, should maintain a relationship with the public that gives reality to the historic tradition that the police are the public and the public are the police, the police being only members of the public who are paid to give full-time attention to duties which are incumbent on every citizen in the interests of community welfare and existence."

PRINCIPLE 8 "Police should always direct their action strictly toward their functions and never appear to usurp the powers of the judiciary."

PRINCIPLE 9 "The test of police efficiency is the absence of crime and disorder, not the visible evidence of police action in dealing with it."

Finally, any leadership development course should include the organization's mission and vision statement. The reason behind the leadership development course is to reiterate the purpose of policing. This is accomplished by stressing loyalty to the profession of law enforcement as opposed to loyalty to an organization or peers that may potentially be engaged in corruption or misconduct. When organizational values are stressed by members at the bottom of the organization in addition to the leaders, eventually the message will take hold, and there will be a shift in the culture.

Leading the Change Process

Managing organizational change is the process of planning and implementing change in organizations by minimizing employee resistance and cost to the organization, while also maximizing the effectiveness of the change effort (George & Jones, 2001). The suggested change process in this section is designed to minimize the cost and risk to employees by actively engaging them in the process. This process of change should be a long-term project. During the process, several short-term goals should be achieved as the organization continues to move forward.

Dismantling the wall of silence should be the objective of every organization and could be considered just as significant as the tearing down of the Berlin Wall. Once the wall is removed, the relationship between the organization and the communities they have taken an oath to serve and protect will be restored and strengthened.

Evaluation of Employee Behavior

The final step in implementing change is the creation of measuring devices that will signify the short-term and long-term success in cultural change. These methods should be developed and agreed upon by a group that comprises various personnel from all levels of the organization. This will create a flat structure that should eliminate some attitudes that may be resistant to any organizational change. The group will determine the metrics and measuring process that will be used to assess the progress of the change project. Additional steps should be taken to map the flow of changes in activities and outcomes at various levels of the organization to ensure the change is taking hold at all levels (Goodman & Rousseau, 2004).

Leader Self-Development

"In the end, it is important to remember that we cannot become what we need to be by remaining what we are." Max De Pree

Individuals that aspire to be leaders should focus a great deal of their efforts on self-development. It is a critical mistake for current and future leaders to rely solely on their organizations' leadership development programs. Many development programs are meant to focus on organizational goals, visions, and missions, but may be influenced by the organization's current culture. To rely solely on an organization's management training programs to produce growth in areas of leadership, may suck you into the organization's leadership vacuum.

Leadership extends outside the physical walls of the organization and into the depths of society. This section of the book provides a foundation for current and future leaders to build a lasting and personalized self-development program.

The Broken Windows Theory of Leadership

The broken windows theory in public safety suggests that if a broken window is left unfixed for a period, it symbolizes disorder and leads to more broken windows, generating increased criminal activity. Let us apply the broken windows theory to leadership and examine how organizational culture can thus lead to a leadership vacuum.

Business consultant Terry Starbucker wrote a blog about the leadership vacuum and titled it, "9 Telltale Signs of a Leadership Vacuum." His list provides the most comprehensive and perceptible behaviors of which every manager should be cognizant (see Appendix C). Leadership vacuums are not necessarily a physical absence of leaders but can be attributed to a lack of leadership skills and organizational awareness.

With hierarchical levels of management in public safety, leadership vacuums can occur at every level. If the broken window is at the frontline supervisor level, how likely will the upper ranks become aware of the problem? Probably not until the problem has taken a toll on the organization. I have witnessed situations in which one employee was engaged in misconduct. Upon further examination of the incident, it was determined that other personnel were engaged in the same behavior. How did the level of misconduct get to the point that it was systemic? The broken windows theory of leadership is the answer. The problem went unfixed for a period, which led to more of the same issues. This is how the leadership vacuum occurs. Leaders are in place, but they are not aware, or do not have the skill set to address the broken windows in their area of responsibility. That is why self-development is paramount to current and future leaders. The astute leader defends against the decay of leadership by being proactive. They see the problem before, or while it is developing. By being proactive, the good leader manages to stay out in front of the problem.

Personal Core Values

An officer working during the September 11, 2001, terrorist attacks in New York City and Washington D.C. relayed a story about leadership in his organization. The officer was assigned to a traffic detail in a city that was not directly impacted by the acts of terrorism. While it was unclear as to what was taking place during those anxious moments, many cities were put on high alert and mobilized many of their public safety forces. This illustration is not designed to make light of those events, but to enlighten management on the importance of personal core values and personal codes of ethics during critical incidents. The officer spoke of how he and other members of the organization were assigned to control traffic at major downtown intersections. Although the traffic lights were operational, the officer assumed the leadership wanted a high concentration of officers in the downtown area to ensure the citizens felt safe. After several hours in the intersection and with no relief, the officer found himself needing to find a restroom. In addition to needing a restroom break, the officer had not had a meal.

The officer asked a coworker that was working another intersection to cover his assignment while he found a place to relieve himself. With most of the businesses closed, the officer eventually made his way to the main police building. As the officer walked through the doors of the building, he smelled what he described as "the aroma of freshly baked pizza." He said he observed many public safety executives eating pizza and enjoying the comforts of an air-conditioned building. Eventually, the officer contacted his wife and asked her to pick up food for him and the officers working the other intersections.

Many will say this is what the officer signed up for, but good leaders will adhere to this General George C. Marshall quote, "When we are tired, cold and hungry, at the end of the day, it is the leader who puts aside his personal discomfort to look to the needs of his soldiers." In this instance, the leadership had an obligation to ensure their personnel were provided relief. There are many sections in this book where this example could have been placed. The story was put in this section because any leader with an internal set of core values will attend to the needs of their personnel.

Personal core values or codes of ethics are those internal values that guide us in our daily journey. Core values become more evident when encountering gray areas and moment decisions. Many leaders have developed their personal core values into a few words that can be recited at any moment. I have personal core values and an individual purpose statement. My personal core values are centered on integrity and credibility. My purpose statement is directed toward helping and serving people on a daily basis.

Internal values are developed early in a person's life. These values determine the manner in which people respond to incidents that occur in the world around them. In essence, internal values guide people in determining how they will respond to life's daily challenges. Personal core values emanate from the center of who we are as human beings and outline what is most important to us as public safety professionals. A leader with no personal core values will often end up besieged by internal conflict. The internal conflict leaves them to wonder why they allowed an injustice to happen, or why they failed to take appropriate action.

Clarified personal core values provide a greater sense of self and establish how people adapt to their environment. When personal core values are not clearly identified, the leader may end up in continual internal and external conflict.

The previous story is an illustration of an officer, who as a leader exhibited personal core values by not only providing for himself, but also providing for those around him. The good leader will always consider others. Those who choose to sit around in comfort while their personnel are out in the field sweating, tired, and hungry do not exhibit good leadership traits. Remember, "rank has its privileges, but not at the expense of subordinates."

A function of a leader is to create, maintain, and improve members in their organization, in order for them to achieve shared objectives (Burke, Macdonald, & Stewart, 2006). When the frontline people are hot, hungry, and tired, they are less likely to achieve their objective. Show people you care, and they will reciprocate loyalty and commitment. Show people you do not care, and they will show you their backside. The officer/leader in the previous story possessed a set of personal core values that would not allow him to see others suffer; he had empathy for those who were encountering the same conditions he was confronting.

Many people develop a set of personal core values as children, and these are often refined as adults. Many people will learn about sympathy, empathy, honesty, and impartiality when they are children. As adults, core values become a part of their character. Many leaders further develop or refine their personal core values during their time spent in the military, college, or religious institutions. The fact that a person has served in the military, attended college, or claims a religious background does not make them above reproach, it is how the person behaves when they have access to power that determines their leadership abilities.

When you have power within an organization, you must maintain your core values because it is in the midst of possessing power that most leaders lose their credibility. Consider the late Kenneth Lay who was the former CEO of Enron; what many people may not know about Kenneth Lay, is that he graduated from the U.S. Navy Officer Candidate School. It is well known that the Navy's core leadership competency models are engrained in their graduates. Accomplishing Mission, Leading People, Leading Change, Working with People, and Resource Stewardship are the competencies that define the expected behaviors of Navy leaders. The core values ensure that leaders in the Navy are effective in their positions. Kenneth Lay understood the importance of leadership, but he allowed greed and personal gain to diminish his personal core values.

To develop personal core values or a personal code of ethics, consideration should be given to one word; that word is LEGACY. Remember, managers leave positions, and leaders leave legacies. What do you want your legacy to be? How do you want your leadership reign to be remembered? When you walk into the room today, what do people say about you? When you leave the room, is there a sigh of relief or a natural desire to remain engaged with you? What will they say one, five, or ten years after you have retired or moved to another position? Mahatma Gandhi once said, "Your beliefs become your thoughts. Your thoughts become your words. Your words become your actions. Your actions become your habits. Your habits become your values. Your values become your destiny."

To develop personal core values, there are many life coaches, who will gladly accept your money to help you in this area. The key to developing core values is to evaluate and reevaluate. If you believe you have personal core values, then take a minute and write them down. If it took you more than sixty seconds to write them down, then you do not have an established set of personal core values. Do you utilize your personal core values in your decision-making?

Strong and effective leadership is about having a set of personal core values and acting on them. Core values are about principles, integrity, authenticity, and being trustworthy. It is about the eagerness to take calculated risks and develop innovative ways of doing things. Finally, it requires audacity and the personal responsibility to stand up for your values and not be afraid to admit when you make mistakes.

For assistance in developing personal core values, there are several core value assessments available on the Internet. The Center for Ethical Leadership has a "Self-guided Core Values Assessment." This assessment is challenging, but that is what makes it preferable for public safety leaders. The assessment will ultimately help every leader, and those that aspire to lead, to clarify their personal core values.

Profiles and Assessments

Over the years, I have taken a multitude of assessments and profiles to measure areas of leadership behavior, emotional intelligence, and decision-making and leadership style. The two that stand out are the Multifactor Leadership Questionnaire: Actual vs. Ought (MLQ A/O) and the Emotional and Social Competency Inventory, University Edition (ESCI- U).

These self-assessment tools have given managers new awareness of behavioral and emotional leadership traits. These assessments often provide confirmation of some of the things you already knew about yourself, and create awareness of those things you did not know. As a leader navigates the process of self-development, it is important to evaluate and develop what they have learned about their strengths and weaknesses through various assessments, reading material, and peer interaction.

The key to self-development is to be completely open and honest in self-assessments and to poll peers and subordinates to determine assessment accuracy. Many people have the belief that they are great leaders, but a quick poll of their people may counter that belief. Denial is the most significant barrier to leader self-development. Individuals that are not interested in hearing constructive feedback from peers or subordinates about their leadership qualities are in denial. Subsequently, these leaders will start to notice the telltale signs of a leadership vacuum that permeates throughout their organization.

Performance appraisals are often given to subordinates by management, but why are subordinates never provided the opportunity to appraise the performance of management. Often it is because management does not particularly care about the opinions or thoughts of subordinates as they relate to leadership or management capabilities. There are occasions when management discards the feedback of their personnel; thus, they miss an opportunity to connect with people. Sometimes as a leader, you have to show people that you are human and that you make mistakes. Own your strengths and your weaknesses and do not be afraid to convey those to others. What is important is that leaders continue to strengthen their strengths and weaken their weaknesses.

Personal mastery is described as a continual learning process. There are certain individuals in public safety organizations that have a desire to enhance the process of personal mastery and have sought various tools outside of the organization in order to meet this goal. Many courses and assessments have assisted many current and future leaders in the area of personal mastery. Self-development provides an opportunity to build on leadership experiences and to create a continuous personal learning environment. Seeking external sources to develop leadership skills shows initiative, dedication, and responsibility, and these efforts will ultimately be rewarded intrinsically and extrinsically.

Conclusion

Imagine if you were preparing for a promotional interview and the topic of leadership came up. By reading this book, you are well prepared to answer questions pertaining to leading an organization well into the 21st century. There are an overwhelming number of books and articles on management, leadership, and supervisory development. This book is slightly different because it is tailored to public safety organizations and is authored by a public safety professional; however, many of the topics in this book can be used in any organizational settings.

There will be people who may disagree with some of the content of *Bridging the Gap*. Just as there will be people that will agree with some of the content. The benefit of disagreement is that it creates the opportunity for conversation and reasonable discussion.

Leaders in organizations must understand that leadership is not a one-size-fits-all approach. It must be tailored to enhance the mission, vision, and purpose of the organization. At the same time, leaders must be willing to develop the skill sets of every member of their organization. *Bridging the Gap* provides a leadership framework for current and future leaders that operate in local, state, and federal public safety agencies. It is the hope that as we proceed through our careers, we establish leadership capabilities that enable us to influence the careers of our peers and subordinates in a positive manner. It is my hope that this book fulfills a great portion of that prospect.

As you close the final page of the book, open up your mind to the many possibilities that lay ahead. You are born a leader, but you must take the time to transform yourself into a great leader!

About the Author

Dr. Anthony Wilson was born and raised in Columbus, Ohio, and currently resides in Grove City, Ohio. Anthony is a proud graduate of the Columbus City Schools system. He obtained his Bachelor of Arts in Leadership from Ohio Christian University. He received a Master of Arts in Human Services/Executive Leadership from Liberty University in Virginia, and his Doctorate in Organizational Leadership from The Chicago School of Professional Psychology, in Chicago, Illinois. Anthony served four years in the United States Air Force as a Security Specialist and is a 25-year veteran of the Columbus, Ohio, Division of Police where he worked as a Patrol Supervisor, Recruitment Supervisor, Crisis Negotiator, and Internal Affairs investigator. He currently serves as an Assistant Chief of Police for the Westerville, Ohio, Division of Police.

Dr. Wilson is available to provide leadership workshops and diversity training to for profit and non-profit organizations. For more information, send an email to acwilson5329@gmail.com

Addendum A: Leadership Styles/Behaviors/Theories

This is not an all-inclusive list of leadership styles, but those listed are the most prevalent methods in public safety organizations. Take a moment to identify the leadership style that best describes you. In addition, try to distinguish the leadership style that is prevalent in your organization, and consider the overall morale of the people in your organization.

Implicit Leadership Theory: Addresses subordinate expectations of leaders and their evaluation of leaders' actions. This is often based on the relevant or irrelevant actions of leaders that directly affect their followers.

Situational Leadership: Developed and studied by Kenneth Blanchard and Paul Hersey. It suggests that the leader or manager of an organization must adjust his or her style to fit the development level of the followers they are trying to influence. Situational leadership maintains that the leader must change his or her style, as opposed to the followers adapting to the leader's style.

Participative Leadership: Is a managerial style that seeks input from employees on all organizational decisions. The employees are given valuable information regarding agency issues, and a majority vote determines the course of action the organization will take. Participative leadership is viewed as a slower form of decision-making and can be utilized for decisions involving changes to units, bureaus, and other groups.

Transformational Leadership: Was strongly influenced by James McGregor Burns. This is a managerial style that develops followers into leaders by responding to individual followers' needs by empowering them and by aligning the objectives and goals of the individual followers, the leader, and the agency as a whole.

Transactional Leadership: Influenced by Max Weber, who believed this was the best style of leadership for bureaucratic organizations. In this managerial style, subordinates are not encouraged to be creative or to find new solutions to problems. Research has determined that transactional leadership can be useful in some situations, but is considered insufficient and may prevent both leaders and followers from achieving their full potential.

Autocratic Leadership: Is also known as authoritarian leadership. This managerial style establishes clear expectations for what needs to be done, when it should be done, and how it should be done. There is also a clear separation between leadership and followers. Authoritarian leaders make decisions independently with little or no input from the rest of the group.

Inclusive Leadership: This managerial style strives to create an environment where employees feel they are part of one organization. Every member's contributions, no matter their title, is valued to better adapt to new opportunities and challenges. Inclusive leaders leverage the diversity of their organizations to address problems and draw on their vast experience to create practical solutions that are directly relevant to members of their community.

Addendum B: Personal Core Values List

Your personal values are the qualities that are most important and meaningful to you. They are typically seen in your actions and the decisions you make.

Select at least five values from the list below, or add words that may not be attached to this list. Once you have chosen your words, take time to narrow your list down to five of the most important values. Look for words that appeal to you and not words that you think other people will relate to you. These words will establish the core values that will guide you throughout your career.

Community	Compassion	Competence
Courage	Empathy	Family
Freedom	Honesty	Integrity
Leadership	Loyalty	Openness
Passion	Peace	Persistence
Purpose	Recognition	Professionalism
Responsibility	Respect	Service
Enthusiasm	Commitment	Accountability

Addendum C: Starbucker's Leadership Vacuum Signs

The flow of bad news stops crossing the executives' desks: Too much good news flowing to the C-suite is a sure signal that the fear factor has kicked in and critical issues needing their attention will be quite late in coming, if at all.

Blank stares (and no nodding heads) at all staff gatherings: It's not usually boredom that causes this to happen (which can be a significant misinterpretation); they've flipped their internal switches to "off" and the words just don't get through—a big sign that the trust bonds are frayed or broken.

More electronic than "real" conversations: Too much e-mail and not enough face-to-face meetings and phone calls indicates a brewing communication problem, as well as a threat of inertia (a big business killer). C'mon folks, if you have to e-mail the person in the next cubicle or office…

Lack of action on problem staff, and the loss of high performers: When the underperformers stick around, and the stars leave, watch out—trouble's a brewin'. This is a huge morality killer.

The rise of "back-channel" communication, venting, and gossip: There is always going to be some of this going on, but if it expands from a trickle to a near flood, the leadership wheels are falling off. There is nothing more uncomfortable than a leader walking into a break room to "Shhhh, he's here…"

Perfunctory meetings: I call it the "mile wide and inch deep" syndrome; we THINK things are getting done in a very orderly and fast way, when, in fact, we're skating briskly over a very shallow pond of "just get it over with" malaise.

People "just doing their job, nothing more": This is a sentence unhappy teammates will utter out loud when things go south (with the actual hope that a leader will overhear it); it's the equivalent of that line in the old TV show "Lost in Space": "Danger, danger, Will Robinson!"

Implementation of the ignorance strategy: When problems fester without action from above, the ignorance strategy is in play—leaders are ignoring them in the hope that they just eventually go away. It is an easy plan to implement, but 99 times out of 100, it will fail with disastrous consequences (and the other one time it was just plain luck).

Misalignment and hidden agendas: Another phrase for this one is "every person for themselves." Silos proliferate, and individual goals and politics take precedence over team and overall goal alignment. A classic example is a sales force caring for nothing more than commissions, leaving customer "messes" behind for the rest of the team to clean up—if they can.

References

Armenakis, A. A., Field, H. S., & Harris, S. G. (1999). Making change permanent: A model for institutionalizing change interventions. Research in Organizational Change and Development, 12, 97-128. doi:10.1016/s0897-3016(99)12005-6

Bass, B. M., & Riggio, R. E. (2006). The transformational model of leadership. In G. R. Hickman (Ed.), Leading organizations: perspectives for a new era (pp. 76-86). Thousand Oaks, CA: Sage Publications

Beer, M., Eisenstat, R. A., & Spector, B. (1990). Why change programs don't produce change. Harvard Business Review. Retrieved from http://webdb.ucs.ed.ac.uk/operations/honsqm/articles/Change1.pdf

Bolton, K. (2003). Shared perceptions: black officers discuss continuing barriers in policing. American Journal of Police, 26(3), 386 – 399.

Bonaventura, L. D. (Producer), & Bay, M. (Director). (2009). Transformers: revenge of the fallen (Motion picture). United States: Paramount Pictures.

Boyatzis, R., & Goleman, D. (2013) ESCI-university edition. Distributed by the Hay Group

Brandl, S. G., & Hassell, K. D. (2009). An examination of the workplace experiences of police patrol officers: the role of race, sex, and sexual orientation. Police Quarterly 12(4), 408–430. doi:10.1177/1098611109348473.

Buhrke, R. A. (1996). A matter of justice: lesbians and gay men in law enforcement. New York, NY: Routledge.

Burke, C., MacDonald, I., & Stewart, K. (2006). Systems leadership: Creating positive organizations. Hampshire, England: Gower.

Burnette, J. L., Hoyt, C. L., & Inella, A. N. (2012). I can do that: the impact of implicit theories on leadership role model effectiveness. Personality and Social Psychology Bulletin, 38, 257-268. doi: 10.1177/0146167211427922

Cameron, K. & Quinn, R. (2011). Diagnosing and changing organizational culture; Based on the competing values framework, (3rd ed.). San Francisco, CA: Jossey-Bass

Dauber, D., Fink, G., & Yolles, M. (2012). Understanding organizational culture as a trait theory. European International Management, 6(2), 199 – 220.

Day, D. V. (2001). Leadership development: a review in context. The Leadership Quarterly,11(4), 581–613.

Dempsey, J. & Forst, L. (2010). An Introduction to Policing, (6th ed). Florence, KY: Delmar Cengage.

Duncan, W. J., LaFrance, K. G., & Ginter, P. M. (2003) Leadership and decision making: a retrospective application. Journal of Leadership & Organizational Studies 9, 1–20. doi:10.1177/107179190300900401

Falkenberg, J., Haueng, A. C., Meyer, C. B., & Stensaker, I. (2002). Excessive change: Coping mechanisms and consequences. Organizational Dynamics, 31(3), 296-312. doi:10.1016/S0090-2616(02)00115-8

Farber, B. J. (2013). Code of silence litigation: Officer use of force. AELE Monthly Law Journal, 1, 101-112. Retrieved from: http://www.aele.org/law/2013all01/2013-01MLJ101.pdf

Finerman, W. (Producer), & Zemeckis, R. (Director). (1994). Forest Gump (Motion picture). United States: Paramount pictures.

Ford, J., Harding, N. (2007). Move over management: we're all leaders now. Management Learning, 38 (5), 475-493.

Frey, D., Kerschreiter, R., Peus, C., & Traut-Mattausch, E. (2010), What is the value? economic effects of ethically-oriented leadership. Journal of Psychology, 218(4), 198-212.

George, J. M., & Jones, G. R. (2001). Towards a process model of individual change in organizations. Human Relations, 54(4), 419-444. doi:10.1177/0018726701544002

Giuliani, R. W. (2002). Leadership. New York, NY: Hyperion

Goodman, P. S. & Rousseau, D. M. (2004). Organizational change that produces results: The linkage approach. Academy of Management Executive, 18(3), 7-19. doi:10.5465/AME.2004.14776160

Greenberg, J. (1996). The Quest for justice on the job: Essays and experiments. Thousand Oaks, CA: Sage Publications.

Hoffman, B. (2012). American icon: Alan Mulally and the fight to save the ford motor company. New York, NY: Random House

Holtzclaw, E. (2014). What most failed leaders have in common. Inc. Retrieved from: http://www.inc.com/eric-v-holtzclaw/what-most-failed-leaders-have-in-common.html

Irahim, Q., Raoof, A., & Rehman, R. (2010). Role of corporate governance in firm performance: a comparative study between chemical and pharmaceutical sectors of pakistan . International Research Journal of Finance and Economics, 50, 7-16.

Judge, T. A., & Robbins, S. P. (2010). Essentials of organizational behavior. Upper Saddle River, NJ: Pearson Education.

Kotter, J. P. (1995). Leading change: Why transformation efforts fail. Harvard Business Review on Point (March-

April), 1-10. Retrieved from: http://csopp.docutek.com/eres/coursepage.aspx?cid=3491&page=docs

Maxwell, J. (1993). Developing the leader within you. Nashville, TN: Thomas Nelson

McDonaugh-Taub, G. (2013). 'Sully' sullenberger: heroism and life after the 'miracle'. Retrieved from: https://finance.yahoo.com/blogs/off-the-cuff/sully-sullenberger-heroism-life-miracle-130336530.html

Mintzberg, H. (2011). Managing. San Francisco, CA: Barrett-Koehler Publishers

Needham, R. (2012). Team secrets of the navy SEALS: The Elite Military Force's Leadership Principles for Business. Manhattan, New York: Skyhorse Publishing, Inc.

Persico, J., & Powell, C. (1995). My American journey. New York, NY: Random House.

Powell, C. (2005). Effective leaders made not born. Stanford Report. Retrieved from http://news.stanford.edu/news/2005/november30/powell-113005.html

Quinn, R. E., & Weick, K. E. (1999). Organizational change and development. Annual Review of Psychology, 50(1), 361-386. doi:10.1146/annurev.psych.50.1.361

Senge, P. M. (2006). The fifth discipline: the art and practice of the learning organization. New York: Doubleday

St. Marie, T. (2012). The 9 telltale signs of a leadership vacuum. Retrieved from: http://www.terrystarbucker.com/2012/07/01/the-9-telltale-signs-of-a-leadership-vacuum/

Yukl, G. (2010). Leadership in organizations (7th ed.). Upper Saddle River, NJ: Prentice Hall.

Made in United States
North Haven, CT
19 August 2024